AF224897

The Grand Prize

And Other Stories from the 1950s

By Raymond Johnson

With

Linda Farris Kurtz

Copyright © 2024

All rights reserved.

All rights reserved. No part of this publication may be reproduced, distributed, or transmitted in any form or by any means, including photocopying, recording, or other electronic or mechanical methods, without the author's prior written permission, except in the case of brief quotations embodied in critical reviews and certain other non-commercial uses permitted by copyright law. For permission requests, please get in touch with the author.

Contents

Dedication

This book is dedicated to the author's parents, Otto and Otelia Johnson, and all their descendents.

Acknowledgments

I would like to thank the members of my Friday afternoon memoir group: Joel Thurtell, Kristyn Huige, and Anne Lechartier. I typed all the stories and read them to my group one by one. They encouraged me to have them published.

About the Author

C. Raymound Johnson, born to a Swedish immigrant family in 1909, wrote these stories in the 1950s while taking a correspondence course. He had no college education and no prior instruction in fiction writing; however, these stories are quite remarkable. The author died in 1991. He left these unusual stories in a box with his daughter, Linda Farris Kurtz.

The Grand Prize

By Raymond Johnson

Aside from one man, who played tunes by blowing across the mouths of empty bottles, and who was subsequently rejected, Mom Stonebreaker was the only entrant over thirty. Her surprise at being accepted, a woman of sixty-eight vivaciously matching her talent with that of youth, was not nearly so great as her feeling of having done something extravagantly foolish.

While she sat in the hotel suite with the other contestants, awaiting the outcome of the radio talent show sponsored by Big Mammy Pig Feed Company, she felt, more than her fatigue, the strain of the wild whirlwind that this incredible day and night had brought into her previously simple, orderly life. For the past hour and a half, she had been wishing she could exchange places with the blower of musical bottles.

"You all know Johnny McQueen, don't you?" Marie Perkins half-shouted from where she was sitting on the divan.

Marie was a singer; that is, she had one of those off-key wails that somehow became popular on the radio and in bars.

Eagles Pernulty, who claimed the ability to imitate any sound, sat on one side of her, and Webster Shivers sat on the other. Webster's arm was half on her shoulder and half on the back of the divan.

"You know Johnny McQueen, Mom?" Marie asked again.

Mom nodded. "He's the one who stole all the votes last year," she said, but Marie could not hear because of the noise the others were making.

"You all know Johnny McQueen?" Marie shouted to the entire room. To Eagles Pernulty, she said, "What a hell of a noisy bunch!"

Mom moved her accordion close to her chair so no one would stumble.

"Who doesn't know him?" said Aberdeen Lovich.

Aberdeen sat on the floor beside Mom's chair, blowing the spit out of the reeds of his clarinet. Mom thought he looked like a wet kitten. He had large brown eyes that appealed for pity of the emaciated face and body, and of the sensitive nature beneath. He had tried so hard to reach the studio audience, which had given him only token applause.

The telephone rang. Mom's eyes sparkled, and her body stiffened.

"That's the first tally, I bet," she said excitedly.

Aberdeen Lovich got up to answer the phone.

"Quiet everybody. This is it." A sudden stillness flattened the atmosphere of the room. "Hello…Yeah, that's right…Too much noise? Sorry…Yeah, OK." He hung up.

The expectancy vanished from Mom's eyes.

"Hotel desk, that's all," said Aberdeen, sitting down again. "We're making too much noise. Quiet down, everybody."

Immediately, the room was refilled by a wild mixture of voices in conversation and laughter.

"Johnny McQueen's a pal of mine," Marie was shouting to everyone, but nobody seemed to care. The rest of Webster's arm had slid down to her shoulders." "He sponsored me on tonight's show. Johnny's a great guy."

Eagles Pernulty said, "He runs this state. Anybody backed by Johnny McQueen is sure to be elected. He's got associated with everything behind him."

"You're not kidding," said Marie. "And Johnny's got them behind me tonight." She laughed shrilly and poked her elbow into Eagles Pernulty's ribs.

Eagles dropped his match folder to the floor. As he bent over to pick it up, his fingers lightly brushed Marie's ankle.

Mom saw everything.

That Pernulty fellow was so bold. He had been fingering Marie ever since they sat down together. Webster Shivers had been openly familiar, too, but he was not so crudely overt as Eagles. Marie's only resistance was a wiggle or the pushing away of a stray hand as if she were merely trying to keep a persistent fly from biting into her flesh.

It was disquieting to Mom. She was not accustomed to a complicated physical situation, and she wished again that Old Joe had, as she had expected him to, set himself against her becoming involved in the Big Mamy Pig Feed radio enterprise.

In the bedroom of the suite, four other contestants were playing canasta, using the bed as a table. Among them was Christine Funkhauser, the coloratura soprano, beautiful, Mom thought, with long golden hair and a soft pink complexion. But those glasses, with the hideous purple plastic frames, gave her the appearance of a deep-water diver in an evening gown. Christine was sweet, with dignity in every move she made, even in the way she called canasta. She was not at all in a class with Marie. She had a background of culture and refinement. That was easy to see. By all standards in judgment of quality, Christine should be the winner of the grand prize.

Marie's voice, wailing, "I used to love you, but it's all over…", punctured the brief pleasure Mom found in the thought.

Eagles Pernulty was fishing for his matches now beside the upper part of Marie's thigh. Marie, without looking, picked up the matches and handed them to him.

"I wish I could get back to Old Joe," Mom said silently, "and forget this whole silly thing."

The baritone voice of Roger Patterson rolled "Old Man River" from the next room. Roger's voice reminded Mom of the sound that came from rubbing a resin-coated string attached to a paper box. Roger was proud of it nevertheless, for every few minutes he pushed "Old Man River" out like long thunder.

Aberdeen Lovich put his clarinet back together and pierced the comparative quiet with an instrumental shriek that vibrated the glass beads in the chandelier.

"Now, she's perfect," he said.

The telephone rang. Aberdeen answered it. When he hung up, he shouted, "Quiet everybody. The house-dick will be up here if we're not quiet."

Eagles Pernulty spoke up in the voice of Andy Brown, "Looky heah, everybody. Quiet down now, like the man says."

Marie laughed. "I could just die when you talk like that."

"Ah, Mamooselle," said Eagles, "coom wid me…"

"Don't he sound just like Sharl Boyay, Mom?" Marie shrieked.

"…coom wid me, and we shall die together," said Eagles.

"He's a card, Mom," Marie laughed. "He can imitate anything."

"Oink, oink," said Eagles, and he tickled Marie's knee.

"Why don't you play for us, Mom?" said Marie. "I love to hear you play. You've got a darned good chance of winning, the way you played 'Dark Eyes'."

"By all means, Madame," said Eagles Boyer; then, with a vicious portrayal of Gary Cooper, he added, "Well, gosh, yes, this here lady knows how to squeeze that box."

Marie giggled. Webster Shivers was beginning to show his jealousy of the Eagles. Webster played piano boogie, and having no piano he could make no bid for recognition.

"Come on, Mom," Marie urged. "Play 'Dark Eyes' for us while we're waiting."

Mom blushed. She tried to think of an excuse to avoid playing. It wasn't that she was afraid of performing in front of people; she'd played at school festivals without any problem. But then Old Joe had been there listening, and it had been for him that she played. Here, she felt, in spite of all the people, every sound her accordion made would be lost in emptiness.

"The hotel may not like it," she said. "I might disturb the other guests."

"Oh, phooey," said Marie. "Everybody likes music."

"Maybe not at eleven o'clock at night," said Mom.

"Just once, Mom," said Marie. "Come on, now, don't be a drip."

Eagles, Webster, and Aberdeen also insisted. Mom felt trapped. With the self-consciousness of a backward amateur, she strapped on her accordion and played "Dark Eyes." Everyone applauded. Christine and Roger remained in the next room, but the other two came out and crowded into positions on the floor. Mom played again. Her face was flushed, and her body quivered with the fear of playing a discordant sound, and when she had finished, she was completely under the spell of that treacherous momentary glory of an admiring audience. Then she played a simple piece called "Whispering Hope" that she had not intended to play, and her fingers caressed the keys of her instrument, and the warmth of her body was breathed into the bellows that swelled each crescendo with vigorous tonal life.

"Oh Joe," she said to herself when the piece ended. "I shouldn't have played that. I didn't mean to play that here."

Everyone in the room was silent for a moment. Then, somehow, they knew that Mom would not play anymore, and suddenly, the beauty of her playing was lost in a meaningless mixture of voices.

Marie swallowed. "Gosh, maybe I won't win after all, even with Johnny McQueen behind me."

At that moment, the door opened to admit a supercharge of nerves in the person of Mr. Chambers, the ideal man for Big Mammy Pig Feed. Marie ran over to him and threw her arms about his neck. He withdrew them with annoyance and consulted the sheet of paper in his hand.

"Now, listen—everybody," he said. "I'm in a hurry. This is the first tabulation. The votes have been coming from every part of the state, so don't ask how your hometown is voting. We can go over that later." He cleared his throat and adjusted his shell-rimmed glasses. "Listen closely. Mrs. Stonebreaker—"

Mom breathed deeply.

"—seven hundred thirty-two. Marie Perkins, six hundred eighty-nine. Eagles Pernulty, six hundred forty-seven. Christine Funkhauser, five hundred ninety-seven."

He read the other names, then backed out of the room. He reopened the door and thrust his head in.

"Incidentally," he said, "the desk asked me to warn you to be quiet."

When he had gone, Marie sat down again between Eagles and Webster. She lit a cigarette.

"Darned close," she said soberly. "Too early to tell anything yet, though. Except for poor Aberdeen. Poor Aberdeen," she teased, "only seventy-two votes."

Aberdeen pouted through his wet sack look of discouragement. "Just wait till they start coming in from St. Looie."

"Mom, you're wonderful," said Marie. "If anybody but me wins, I hope it's you."

Christine Funkhauser passed daintily in front of Mom, gathering up her long, flowing skirt. She gave Mom a playful pat on the cheek and smiled at her through her striking, purple-framed glasses. Then she continued toward the bathroom.

Mom looked after her with motherly affection. She was a sweet girl. Marie could be sweet, too, if she were not so boisterous and crude, and if she would not let those boys finger her so much. Mom did not think Marie could win. She hoped Christine would.

She knew, of course, that she would not win. An old woman simply had no appeal. There was no magic in her name, no history of art, no stage tricks to capture affection. Her votes represented almost the entire adult population of her hometown, and she could expect no more. She was willing to concede to anyone if she could only go home to Old Joe and go to bed and forget this bizarre day.

The ladies of Dorcas could be thanked for the ridiculous situation. The idea had intrigued her; it was true, and the grand prize had excited her, but common sense had overruled them.

"No, I won't make a ninny of myself," she had said.

The ladies of Dorcas and the businessmen of the town pooled their efforts to persuade her. She had to rely on Old Joe to discourage the movement, but to her amazement, he opposed her. He said he did not care about the grand prize, but he would like the satisfaction of hearing an old lady make monkeys out of impersonators and beer parlor howlers.

Mom had no interest in such an accomplishment. If there was a remote hope of winning, she wanted to win the grand prize. She had no use for the yellow convertible, or the year's supply of pig feed, but she wanted the television set for Old Joe and the twelve hundred dollars. Half of it would pay the balance on the house, and the other half would take her and Joe on a nice trip if they were careful. Joe was seventy, and it was time he had a rest.

"What do I want a rest for?" he had said. "You win the money, you keep it. Buy yourself a fur coat to go with the yellow Jenny buggy.

Christine Funkhauser came out of the bathroom, gave her another weird smile, and returned to the canasta game.

It was like Joe to talk that way. Of course, he was tired. Who could help being tired at seventy when he has worked so hard as Joe?

He would welcome a restful trip when the time came. He had never been away from the town where they had lived all their lives. Nor had she, for that matter, except for the few days after she and Joe were married when she went to her grandmother's funeral. Joe had looked so desolate that night when she got on the train.

Now, do be very careful, Mom," he had said, and there was such deep sorrow in his voice that she could not help crying.

It was the same when she left him this time. For days he had boasted how well he would get along without her, how much he would enjoy the peace and quiet during her absence. But as she kissed him goodbye at the depot, his old face took on a forlorn, boyish look, and she knew he'd be lost and helpless in her absence.

Don't play 'Whispering Hope', Mom. That brought you to me, and I'll be waiting for it to bring you back."

Marie was singing, "Cupid shot his arrow, and he had perfect aim…" and Eagles, with his hair down in his eyes, and a vacuous look on his face, played an imaginary piano whose bass clef was located strategically on Marie's knee. Aberdeen Lovich slipped from his sulk long enough to snarl an accompaniment with his clarinet. Webster Shivers had slid his arm boldly around Marie's neck and pulled her head down to rest on his shoulder.

When they had finished, Marie howled with delight. "Old Man River" flowed like glue from the bedroom just as Christine Fankhauser's coloratura called "Canasta!"

Mom applauded Marie's song, although she thought it was hideous. And Eagles was a little fool. She wondered why impersonators and singers like Marie were so popular. Christina deserved many more votes than she had received.

As if propelled by some unseen force, Mr. Chambers burst into the room. His hair was tousled, his necktie had been loosened, and his collar opened.

"Telegrams by the bale now," he shouted. "It's terrific. Now, listen, everybody. Mrs. Stonebreaker, seventeen hundred forty-one—"

Oh, no, Mom thought. There must be some mistake.

"Marie Perkins," said Chambers, "Seventeen hundred twelve."

Marie squealed and clapped her hands. "Good old Johnny McQueen," she cried.

"Christine Funkhauser, nine hundred eight-seven—"

Mr. Chambers read the other names, ending with Aberdeen Lovich, whose score now was a miserable two hundred votes.

"Most of those were from St. Louis," Mr. Chambers declared as he backed out of the room.

Aberdeen struck the floor with the bell of his clarinet and uttered a vile epithet.

Over the shock of his speech, Mom felt sympathy for Aberdeen. His music was his blood. He had spent his youth and earnings trying to imitate Benny Goodman. Mom thought perhaps it would have been better if he had tried harder to be Aberdeen Lovich. Still, his efforts had been worth more than two hundred votes. There was Marie, who probably had not spent a dime on music and doubtless had done her practicing while sitting on some boy's lap. Of course, Johnny McQueen…

Her own popularity was unaccountable. She had practiced, but she had not taken a music lesson since her father junked the old pump organ. And she certainly didn't have a Johnny McQueen to back her up. Only Old Joe and the ladies of the Dorcas Society, Old Joe and his cherished "Whispering Hope." She wished she had not betrayed him by playing it for Marie.

"Seventeen hundred forty-one—" It was exciting to dare to hope. It was ridiculous, like a flimsy movie plot, but it was possible. Oh, no, it was nonsense to think it possible. Marie lagged by only thirty votes, and if Johnny McQueen controlled her votes as he did the election ballots, she would win by a great margin. On the other hand, it was past eleven, and most of the heavy voting should be over—

She should not urge herself into facing a vast disappointment later. The best she could expect now was a second prize, a complete set of beautiful airplane luggage, something she could shove under the bed and forget.

No one had planned for an old woman to win—yellow convertible, pig feed, airplane luggage. But she longed for no prize at all from the Big Mammy Pic Feed Company. She was tired; the gold plate had been worn off by the event that had lured her from her well-regulated life, and all she really desired was home and Old Joe and the feel of his clumsy arms around her.

She wished she could give her votes to Christine. Christine was such a good loser, so unselfish. It surely was not easy to know a lovely voice could not be rewarded.

Mr. Chambers had coffee and sandwiches sent up, and everyone gathered in one room for refreshment. Mom sat near Christine.

"I admire your composure," Mom said. "You're not at all excited by the voting."

Christine smiled, and turned her large, purple-framed eyes upon Mom.

"Darling, I've been through this before, many, many times. I never win."

Mom gave her a puzzled look.

"This way, you see," said Christine, adjusting the lettuce on her sandwich, "I know I have a large audience. And there are a few charming people I meet—like you and Roger Patterson."

At that moment, Roger surprised everyone by rolling out "Wagon Wheels" instead of the river. When the sandwiches and coffee were finished, he and Christine returned to the bedroom to play two-handed rummy.

Marie was brushing crumbs from her skirt. Eagles Pernulty imitated a monkey, picking up a crumb and nibbling it with the finesse of a practiced rhesus. Webster Shivers crowed with childish glee.

The door opened suddenly, and a large man with a crooked nose crowded into the room.

"I'm the house officer," he said hoarsely. "You've been warned to keep quiet. Now, if I have to come up here again, you'll all go out on your ear." He turned a bullish look around the room and withdrew.

"Ugly son-of-a—" Marie said to the closed door, then held her nose and made a pulling motion in the air.

Webster laughed again, and Marie and Eagles chuckled together.

Mom was deeply humiliated. The house officer had looked at her as he spoke. She felt as if she had been accused of being part of an immoral combine. She was trapped amid an undesirable element, with no means of escape until morning.

Mr. Chambers returned at midnight. His voice was dry and raspy from answering phone calls. He reviewed his latest report: Marie and Mom were tied at seventeen hundred fifty votes.

Marie gave a prolonged cry of hysterical delight and pounded her knees. "Good old Johnny McQueen. I love that guy."

Mom shifted restlessly in her chair. "Why," she asked herself, "in the name of common sense, must this go on and on?" She made a silent plea to Johnny McQueen to hasten the barroom votes so her nightmare would end.

Mr. Chambers purposely avoided reading the other names, vanishing before Aberdeen Lovich could inquire if any more St. Louis votes had come in.

Marie was in a paroxysm. Mom could not tell if it was because she knew Johnny McQueen or because she had approached so near victory.

She was reckless in her jubilation. Webster's right arm entwined her, so his hand fitted snugly beneath her breast. His left hand was on the bare flesh about the knee.

Mom could contain herself no longer. "Marie, dear, your dress has slipped up."

It was a feeble beckoning of decency. Marie idly folded her dress down to her knee but let Webster's hand remain. Mom looked about for a means of diverting her attention. Everyone else was, in his own manner, nursing his wound of defeat. Aberdeen Lovich was compensating for his loss in the violent action of a Superman Comic. Mom thought perhaps she could find a way to talk to Christine. She was shocked momentarily when she looked toward the bedroom and found it dark. Then Christine appeared, composed and beautiful as ever, except for her purple eyes, and gracefully crossed the floor to the bathroom.

"Darling, you're wonderful," she said to Mom in passing, "to put up with this gaucherie." She cast a disdainful look at Marie.

When Mr. Chambers came back again, he appeared desolated by the weariness climaxing the promotion of Big Mammy Pig Feed contests. Marie had gained nearly two hundred votes, Mom only ten.

"Oh, thank heavens!" Mom cried to herself and covered her face with her hands.

Marie threw her arms and legs up, pivoting her body on her haunches. She threw her head and arms across Webster's lap and flung her legs across those of Eagles Pernulty, who seized the opportunity to fondle them by strumming them as he would the strings of a guitar.

"Oh, I love that guy," Marie howled. "Dear, darling Johnny McQueen."

Mom rose suddenly from her chair. There was no place to go, except into the hall, and she feared meeting the house officer there, but she felt she had to do something in protest of the exhibition.

Roger Patterson came over and took her hand in his.

"Mom, you're admirable, simply admirable," he said with a toothy, klieg-light smile, "to put up with this – this—"

"Gaucherie," Mom snapped.

"Precisely, dear, precisely," said Roger, and he proceeded to move about the room, like a large ant, aimlessly inspecting its other occupants.

Mom sat down again.

Marie sang loudly her praise of Johnny McQueen while Webster Shivers combed her hair with his fingers, and Eagles Pernulty removed her shoes.

"Oh, Joe Stonebreaker," Mom cried out silently, with secret anguish. Why did you let me do this!"

The atmosphere in the room felt stifling, thick with the shamelessness and shallowness of little people.

When the knock sounded at the door, Mom almost leaped forward to answer. Her mind and spirit clawed for escape from Marie and Eagles and the almighty Johnny McQueen and Webster Shivers. She flung the door open. Her eyes filled with tears as she stared into the face of Old Joe Stonebreaker.

He wore a little boy look designed to discourage scolding.

"Thought you might be lonesome, Mom." He said to hide his own longing. "Had Elsie Collins drive me down to keep you company."

Mom reached up and wrapped her arms around his big neck, "Oh, Joe, Joe, Joe."

She turned and looked with triumph at the faces of the Big Mammy Pig Feed contestants, and as she turned, Roger Patterson, with the stealth of a leopard but a second off in timing, stepped into the bathroom.

Mom felt a drop of bitterness touch her heart, then a sudden pity for Christine and somehow, quite abruptly, Marie's gaucherie became less ugly.

"Joe, we must go right away," she said. "Take me away, Joe, anywhere; I can't stay here another minute."

Marie, a picture of scrambling legs and arms, pulled herself to a sitting posture.

"But, Mom, you've got to stay and congratulate me when I get the grand prize."

Mom took hold of Old Joe's big hand and hugged it closely. Marie could have her yellow convertible, her pig feed, her television set and the twelve hundred dollars. She held the prize, the grand prize. But Marie, she knew, could not understand that.

The End

An Appointment in Jefferson Street

By Raymond Johnson

For the first time in three years, Gerald Fernigan was to see Holly Samuels. He did not know quite what his reaction would be. He loved her, of course. There had not been a day in thirty years when his love could not be separated from every other feeling in him and positively identified. There had been a few years – they seemed long ago now – sensitive, immature years when he had tried desperately to believe that love for a woman without possession of her could not endure. He thought he had convinced himself of this when suddenly he was overwhelmed by a strong, unreasonable feeling that he did, in some indefinable way, possess her. And there was the feeling, too, vigorous but experimental, that she was fully aware of it. It charged their appointment this afternoon with so much more significance than any previous meeting had possessed.

His taxi reached Jefferson Street, and he dismissed it at the corner so he could walk to her house. He limped a few steps, then paused to study the old, unwashed faces of the houses that looked distrustfully at each other through tangled stray branches of the tired, aged elms that grayed the street with the premature evening.

He did not believe in designs, yet his being here now seemed part of a scheme which had been carefully drawn. He discarded the thought at once. Holly was a wise woman, capable of scheming and playing with lives, but she possessed nothing of cruel cunning. Even when young she had shown wisdom uncommon to girls her age.

Because of it, he had been able to draw far away from himself, the miserable little self he could not have escaped alone. She had clung to him; it was true. She had not forced him to recognize the futility of his love, and even after he knew she was beyond his reach, she did not suggest the painful platitude of a friendly relationship. She had known his intense passion for her and how stupid it would have been of her to expect the tumult of his emotion to simmer down to a holiday friendship. She had clung to him, but not because she had planned to hold him against the time; he could fill the emptiness of fruitless years.

He wondered if he should dare to think so. She had held to Jefferson Street. She had loved it, left it and then returned; surely, there had to be a reason for her return. Or could it be that she'd only recently understood what Jefferson Street meant to her, something she'd overlooked during the years she'd been gone? And maybe, without even realizing it, she needed Gary Fernigan as much as he needed her.

She had said it once, almost. "You seem to be so near when I'm facing a crisis." Perhaps it was the source of her courage when she was compelled to face a crisis: Everything is going to be all right; Gary will come, and everything will be all right.

"Gary will take care of everything," he said involuntarily to himself. He had not called for the thought. It had been lying somewhere deep in him, a bruised remnant of the self-pity with which his adolescence had comforted itself, and it fell into consciousness like the discovery of some long-forgotten keepsake whose significance had corroded with time. He wondered if it could have been her thought when Fulton died in Rome. She had known he was near there. When he cabled that he would arrange all the formalities of returning Fulton's body, her reply simply phrased her gratitude, but more than that, it brought him her smooth, rich voice to speak her own words, "I depend so much upon you, Gary." And while her husband's body lay waiting to go back to her, Gary felt again that he possessed some treasured part of Holly Samuels which Fulton never had known.

He walked slowly toward her house, his lame foot scraping the rough concrete of the sidewalk, which had heaved and cracked over the irrepressible vigor of the giant elm roots working with slow violence toward the sustenance of their upper massiveness. Jefferson Street. Here his life had begun, when he was seventeen, and thereafter it had been a street of enchantment. This afternoon, it bore a look of midsummer sadness, of neglect, of age, of change. Holly's father had built this street, and had planned it to be the most enduring, the nicest semi-aristocratic street in town, immune to time, unaffected by the implacable growth of the city. But it had not endured. Now it was given over almost entirely to the vulgarity of boarding-houses, establishments of light-housekeeping rooms, offices and parlors of chiropractors, and funeral homes, which, despite their gaudy neon signs, retained for the street, with their neat creeping-bent lawns and fresh-painted fronts, a portion of its past dignity.

Before and on either side of each house had been broad, gently sloping lawns giving the appearance of a vast garden of bluegrass, formal arrangements of hedge and shrubbery, with flower beds splashing seasonal color against a rich green background of ewe and juniper. White latticework gleamed between the branches of climbing roses, the abundant foliage of honeysuckle, and the long serpentine stems of wisteria.

Now what arbors remained were crooked, paintless, rotted and purposeless, and the bluegrass, starved and consumed by grubs, had been replaced by rank grasses and chickweed, the ewe and juniper had submitted to drought and red spider, and the hedges of regal privet, lilac and spiraea had become immense masses of tangled growth, coarse, knotted, insect-ridden wood heavily burdened by great patches of brown death.

Gary Fernigan cherished the memory of his first visit to Jefferson Street. He had come into it noisily and furiously late in the afternoon, driving the delivery wagon from Margolis's grocery store, and when the galloping horse's iron-shod hoofs first assaulted the pavement, he drew rein and brought the horse to a standstill. It was the most splendid street he had ever seen. It was the most splendid street in the world. It was the dream he had always tried to dream, with form and substance. Jefferson street…

The street in which he lived had no name. It was a mud flat hugging the river bank near the juncture of Adams Creek and the great sewer, which vomited half the city's filth into the dark, steaming stream of pollution. It was a hideous brown expanse of damp, rotten soil where even the rankest of weeds refused to live, where only the niggers, the hunkies, the shabby Irish could make a feeble bid for survival amid coal ashes, rusty cans and the poisonous fungus of poverty.

He escaped it only in his dreams, taking his mother with him on flights of lightning speed into fields of green or into the high towers of vague, nameless, non-existent castles. Jefferson Street tied his dreams to reality, and he sat on Margolis's wagon, stunned, oblivious to all but the sweet-pitch smell of the clean asphalt pavement, the soft, tender sound of leaves kissing, and the cool shade of the elms, and as he carried a box of groceries to the rear of Holly's house he dreamed, seeing nothing until he reached the great immaculate kitchen, impressive with its immensity and cleanliness of white enamel and porcelain and tile, where Holly stood with her Aunt Ellen.

Oh, that awful, deadening shyness that washed over him when he came face to face with the girl—the way his knees and arms trembled uncontrollably, leaving him as weak and hollow as an empty paper bag whenever she locked eyes with him and didn't look away. All the moisture in him seemed to rush to the palms of his hands, leaving his throat dry as cotton. She was young, at least two years younger than he, but she was tall, and her strength and vigor showed in every arc that formed the features of her face and in the shape of her fingers. She stood straight, her hands on her hips, and she seemed so much stronger than he was with his scrawny body and lame foot, making him more conscious than ever of his physical inadequacy.

"You must be the new boy from Mr. Margolis's," the older woman said. "I hope you're better than the last."

Better than the last. Vulgar, clumsy, devastatingly shy, born in a sewer, waking always to dead morning. Was that better?

The girl said nothing, but she looked at him so steadfastly, with much intense, searching eyes, eyes too knowing for a girl of fifteen, that even when he turned his face away to hide its embarrassment, he could see her in his mind looking at him. And when he returned to his wagon, the look followed him and he felt deeply and sadly and fiercely his own scrubby ugliness.

Jefferson Street would always be only a dream. It was for people like this girl, not for clumsy, struggling grocery clerks, stinking of dirty blood on a butcher's apron.

"Why did I have to see her? Why did I have to come here?"

He whacked the horse across the rump, and forced it on faster and faster with continued brutal whacking until he was again out of Jefferson Street.

But he could never force the girl's look out of his mind. Wherever he went to deliver Margolis's wares, no matter into whose kitchen, he always entered the kitchen that held the girl Holly, and all the other people he saw, namable but indescribable, were visible only as eyes, mouths, noses, hair, ears, chins, moles, scars, smiles, frowns, smirks, so many scattered parts, never integrated, for always there was the face of Holly to see and to prevent their coming together in any significant form.

This girl was so strong, so alive, with eyes that tore into his so deep that all his faults were laid bare for him to see, filled him with frustration and an overpowering desire to dig hard and deep into some great endeavor, some vast, profound task no human effort before had succeeded to perform. The feeling drove him from the confinement of Margolis's store even when there were no deliveries to make, and it was the more furious when he set upon the wagon, and he grasped the reins firmly, digging his feet into the worn, splintered wood of the buckboard, to keep from hurling himself into space. He was in love. With the violence of youth, he was in love, not only with a girl who possessed the strength and perfection of form he longed to possess, but in love with a street, a score of houses, with a way of living that he could not think about without feeling a terrible aching, with a dream that was real as the hardness of granite yet elusive as gossamer. If he could shed this body which gave him only movement, only voice and sound and sight, and reach down into the turmoil of the secret, tormented youth, perhaps he could know with a knowledge nowhere attainable the mystery of its cries and find direction for his furious passion. Each time he saw the girl, the fire in him became more intense. When he made deliveries to the house and did not see her, a furious hunger joined the fire in its effort to destroy him.

He came to hate such days, and he hated himself, his past, and he hated Margolis's little store, and the miserable shack on the stinking river bank. On a Sunday morning, he made up his mind never to go back to any of it. He went from his church to a street on a hill, a paved street where no foul mud could wash, where the smells of the river could not reach, and he rented two rooms and a kitchen, though he had no idea what he would use for rent money. Then he went to Mr. Margolis, waking him from his Sunday afternoon nap, and quit his job. When he left Margolis, he began his two-mile walk to Holly's house, and he had so much time to think about what he had done that every step he took built fear upon fear. As he neared the girl's house new terror formed in him. How would he find the courage to face her? He had no reason for coming, no groceries to deliver; he had no right to crawl out of his sewer and force himself uninvited into the serenity of Jefferson Street on a Sunday afternoon. The girl would laugh at him. She would shriek in mockery with the cruelty of a girl who has no way of knowing the unfathomable depths of a boy's love.

He was grimy from wind-blown street dust, drenched in sweat, his shirt a damp mess, and his hair sticking to his forehead and ears in unruly strands. Oh, why had he come? Why had he let his foolish thoughts lead him here, only to be ridiculed? Isn't it enough that a boy endures the torment of his thoughts, the pain of his ignorance, and the agony of his inner turmoil?

If he turned away now, he could only go back to the river shack and never again, would he have the courage to come this far. He would be forever a useless cripple inhabiting the sewers of the city.

She was alone, lying in the hammock suspended in the shade of the rose arbor. He went up to her, trembling, cold and wet and trembling, and he knew his tongue would be paralyzed when he tried to speak. She sat up and faced him, and then she smiled.

He was dumb. His jaws hung apart, but his lips were frozen. It was terrible. He could not stand forever and only stare at her.

"I – I was in the neighborhood, "he stammered. He was amazed to find his voice did not tremble. His tongue was easily commanded. The shaking in him had stopped. "That isn't true," he said. "I had to come." The cold of his dread vanished. "I had to come because I'm not going to deliver groceries anymore, and I'll probably never see you again."

She did not laugh. She said she was glad he had come, that it did not matter if he came without groceries, and when he sat down on the grass, she sat down beside him. This spot of shade was an endless garden, a whole universe to him, and with her beside him, he felt a strength and vitality he had never known before. He had done, without knowing the moment for it had come, the thing he was meant to do.

There were long months when he could not see Holly. September to Christmas, January to June, while she was away at school, the days were long, restless, and the work he did consume only his energy, leaving his mind whole and free to dwell upon her. At night, he read, trying to study in a haphazard fashion, the books he took from the library, books he did not understand but which he knew he must devour. He searched wildly, aimlessly, for the food his mind must have. There were the philosophies, the wisdom, the labors of tortured minds and driven souls of the ages in compact, stuffy contiguity with the dead, meaningless, valueless, sterile, bloodless, infirm contributions of centuries of bigotry and ignorance. How do you tell which part of the millions upon millions of words would only deaden him, lead only further into frustration and more bitter hunger? There was no designated, all-knowing person on duty within the musty walls of the old library building to guide him. There was no warning word and no counsel inscribed upon the countless catalog cards to tell which book to read, and which not to read. There was no way of telling. But he must know, he must find the answer that would make of him a creature risen above the sewer of his birth, above the dirt, the ignominy of his surroundings, his deeds, he lacks, a creature risen to the wealth symbolized by Jefferson Street. So, he studied, night after night, trying to make himself better for the next time he confronted Holly.

When she was home, she let him come frequently, but there were so many times he could not see her. She went to parties he could not attend, and when she gave parties, he was not asked. He knew it was because she was wise. He would not have blended with her friends on Jefferson Street. The two of them went alone on early Sunday morning picnics. These were far lovelier than parties. He had to share her with no one but the shadows of Brighton's Woods, the squirrels, and the great walnut trees that surrounded them. Usually, they played like children, running and chasing and hiding from each other, and when thoroughly exhausted, they sat down to rest and eat the lunch they brought with them.

One Sunday morning, Gary would not let her run from him. He caught her hand and pulled her to the ground. His face was earnest.

"Holly, you're seventeen," he said. "In a few years, you'll be out of school. What will you do then?"

"I don't know," she replied with equal seriousness. "Father and mother have ideas, but I think I'll do as I please when the time comes." She looked at him teasingly, changing the mood of the moment. "Maybe I'll go to China as a missionary."

He tried to smile. "And I'll go as a—a—I don't know. I haven't learned to be anything."

"I think you would make a good scientist, Gary," she said, and that morning, he knew where to look for the books he was to read.

When Holly turned twenty, her father passed away. Her mother, who had always been emotional, couldn't cope with the sudden challenges she faced. With her aunt out of town, it was up to Holly to handle all the funeral arrangements. Gary stayed by her side throughout.

"I don't know what I'd have done without you," she told him when it was all over. "You're very kind, Gary."

He did not see her for the remainder of that summer. Fulton Samuels, who had been a friend of her father's, was at the house a great deal. Gary made himself wretched with the thoughts that plagued him.

"You're pretty fond of Fulton, aren't you," he said to Holly the first time he saw her after Fulton had gone.

"He is very considerate," she said. "He has become quite famous with his lectures, and I think I admire him very much."

She was sitting in a garden chair, watching the reflection of the evening sun spray first one color and then another through the chains of Autumn clouds. A stray yellow leaf floated down from a tree and rested on her hair. Gary reached to take it off, but instead, he laid his hand softly upon her head.

"Holly," he said; then suddenly he was breathless. He should not have touched her. He had always known that once any part of him met her physically, all his reserve would vanish.

He flung himself down beside her chair, grasped her hand and held it hard against his cheek.

"Holly, I love you. I have loved you so much since the first time I saw you."

Perhaps he had acted so suddenly, or she was too startled to know what to do, but her hand did not draw away. He held it a few seconds, and then his overwhelming shyness swept over him, and he released it. He struggled to draw his wasted foot from under him and rose to his knees.

"I'm sorry," he said. "I'm a fool. I have no right to talk like that. But I couldn't stand the thought of losing you to Fulton."

When he left her, he knew she would one day marry Fulton. She had never said, had never implied that she loved Fulton. But Fulton was a famous man, much older but famous, and she was attracted to him because of his age and brilliance. Was it reasonable to think she would prefer a stupid cripple with a name like Fernigan? She had never said, but he knew. She had never said anything about the way she was inside toward him or anyone else. He tried to make her tell him.

It was a chilly night, and she sat on the divan by the fireplace. The flames cast the room's only light, highlighting her features against the swirling, dark shadows. He intentionally aimed to wound her with his words.

"Jefferson Street crust is so thick on you that nothing can come out. Why do you let me come? You know I don't belong here, yet you let me keep on coming. Why, Holly?"

"I like you, Gary."

"Like me," he said, standing in front of her. "You like dogs, too, and horses—"

"Sit down, Gary," she said quietly.

He sat down beside her. She laid her head against the back of the divan.

"I let you come because I want you to. If I didn't, I could hurt you and make you stay away. I've never wanted to do that, Gary."

"You know how I feel now," he said. "Does that make any difference? I can't keep coming—feeling this way – unless you feel the way I do. That's impossible, isn't it? Even if you tried, feeling this way would be impossible. What else can I do but feel? I have nothing to offer you. I study, I search, and I fumble around in the mess I call my laboratory, but I only grasp the most basic concepts. I have nothing, I know nothing, absolutely nothing—except that I love you, Holly.

"The most elementary things," she said, without looking at him. "no one knows more than that. Everything is elementary to the next step."

"That isn't the sort of talk I want to hear from you, Holly. Do you love Fulton, Holly?"

She did not answer him. He watched the reflection of the fire in her eyes.

"Do you love Fulton, Holly?

Her silence was torture. His eyes fed upon her lips, her throat. He took hold of her hand and pushed his mouth hard against it.

"I love you, Holly."

"Kiss me, Gary," she said.

He brushed her cheeks with his lips.

"On the mouth," she said.

When his lips crushed against hers, every cell in his body stirred fiercely.

"Take me in your arms, Gary."

He held her tightly against him. "Oh, Holly, Holly," he whispered, and he covered her cheek, her throat, her eyelids with kisses. "You love me. Say you love me, Holly."

She did not say it.

"Holly, tell me you love me."

Over and over, he begged her.

"I want to give you this night, Gary."

"You love me, Holly. Tell me."

"This night is yours, Gary."

"Say you love me."

"Take this night, Gary."

It was all she would say. In the heat of his embrace, his mind only half heard her words; half knew their meaning. She would not say she loved him, and suddenly, a cruel, hideous idea seized him. He leaped away from her and stood in the center of the room.

"I know," he cried. "It's this foot. You hate this ugly, horrible foot. You hate it. You're afraid you'll have to face its twisted, ugly nakedness, and you hate it."

"No, Gary." She said, and there were tears on her cheeks, holding the flames of the fire as she protested. "It's not true, Gary."

He fled with violent jerks of his body to the darkness of the porch, down the steps and into the street, limping hurriedly, with the haste of anger and frustration, a ridiculous figure in a lopsided race under the pale lamplight. As he fled, her words poured ceaselessly through every channel of his brain, "Take this night, take this night, this night, this night…Take me, take me, take me…" Why? So he could get the vain, foolish passion out of his system and then go away forever, and she could forget him completely?

The following winter Holly was married to Fulton Samuels and moved away from Jefferson Street.

Well, that part of his life was over. Whatever came now, if anything, would have its basis in his books, in the little facts he was beginning to discover for himself in his makeshift laboratory. What was it she had said? All things are elementary, or something like that. Everything is elementary to the next step; that was it. Well, he had learned a great deal from his feelings toward her. He had needed to feel something besides his awareness of himself. A scientist must feel, must sense a reaction before it manifests itself. All he had felt before was the tremendous weight of inadequacy.

From Holly he had learned how to direct himself. Because of her, he had found the courage to leave the sewers of Adams Creek. He was learning how to weigh values, and it was not done with the names of streets or with the shapes of feet. Holly had planted a good seed. He had one enormous regret—that he had left her like a silly, childish grocery clerk instead of a man of twenty-three.

It was Fulton who brought him face-to-face with Holly again seven years later. He was obsessed with the idea that the sewage of great cities would destroy humanity. Water conservation had become a passion. Water pollution and the threat of bacterial poison it held always existed as a terrifying enemy. He dreamed of the day his own city would erect great sewage plants and free its rivers. He wrote clumsy reports packed with facts and made a nuisance of himself at city-council meetings. He made bacterial tests of the water from the river near which he had lived as a boy and shocked himself when he found evidence of enough poison to kill a hundred thousand men. He always wished he knew more about what he was doing and how to do it. Perhaps if he knew only a little more, the paralysis of limbs and feet and rheumatic fever could be made to vanish. All his work rewarded him with nothing. It was difficult to convince people of dangers they could not see or feel. So long as clean water came from the tap and no foul odors filled the atmosphere, there was no cause for becoming lathered about sewage. How can a mind be troubled by a diminishing water table when the country is plagued by floods every spring?

Fulton Samuels discovered the value of his reports while studying material for a new series of lectures. He also discovered that Gary was so desperately in need of funds that meals were being missed with unhealthy regularity.

"It's time you were getting acquainted with Lucy Valever," he said to Gary. "She's at our place a great deal. Very rich and extremely generous in the promotion of worthy causes."

"I don't even know that this is a worthy cause," said Gary. "If I can prove the merit of what I'm doing, I won't need Lucy Valever."

"Everyone needs a Lucy Valever," said Fulton. "Besides, you have to eat while you're proving, don't you?"

Reluctantly he promised to attend a party at which Lucy Valever would be present, later wishing he had not. He wished Fulton had not found him. He could not think of Fulton and remained detached entirely from Holly. He had made himself believe that Holly's part of his life had ended, that nothing could occur to revive it. Meeting Fulton made him realize the stupidity of his conviction. Fulton was quite gray now, and balding, and he did not belong in the picture his mind carried of Holly.

He dreaded the party. He was even shabbier than he was the last time Holly had seen him, and he did not want her to see how completely he had failed to make the elementary things lead to something better. Fulton's house would be bursting with intellect. He did not belong there any more than he had as a grocery boy in Jefferson Street. He made up his mind not to go; then, he remembered that he was learning a better method of weighing values.

The Valever woman was enormous, conspicuous not only because of her size but because she wore her wealth in extremely bad taste all over herself. Looking at her, one expected to see great wads of money clutched in her fat fingers. It was easy to see why she attended parties like Fulton's. She was buying her way among people who included her only because she could afford the fare. She spoke in a shocking tone, almost crying out to everyone in the room, making her presence constantly known. She enjoyed making verbal thrusts because she knew everyone about her dared not to be offended.

Gary hesitated to talk to her, and when he did, he felt that he had thrust himself into a horrible nightmare.

"Sewers!" She did not speak, she shrieked. "Sewers! Oh my God. Right here in Fulton's living room. Homer – Allen—Listen, everybody. Here's a man who isn't writing a book. He's building sewers. Let me tell you this…" Everybody laughed with dear Lucy. "Sewers…sewers…sewers…"

The room closed in on him, smothering him. He tried to shut the sound of her voice from his brain. He looked about for an easy means of escape. Holly was watching him from across the room. She appeared to be as shocked as he. When he started to leave, she met him at the door.

"I'm sorry, Gary," she said. She clutched his arms, as if to hold him back. In her eyes, there was an intensity that reminded him of the way she first looked at him.

"It's my fault," he said. "My blundering way, that's all. A man shouldn't approach a rich old woman he had never seen before and start talking about sewers as if they were Pomeranians."

"Come back soon, Gary. Fulton is interested in what you're doing."

He did not go back, but Fulton spent much time with him when he was in town. He began making progress. Through Fulton, he met people who understood the meaning of his work. Fulton edited what he wrote, condensed it, and succeeded in publishing enough material to attract respect for his authority. Though his own city ignored him, others invited him to make studies of their sewage systems. While he was away on such a mission, he received word that Holly had given birth to a son.

The news profoundly affected him, leaving him stunned. He had never imagined Holly with a child. He felt a deep mix of resentment, envy, and jealousy toward Fulton. Despite these feelings, he couldn't stay away and visited her the day she came home.

"You seem to be so near when I'm facing a crisis," she told him. Fulton had been unable to reach home, his plane having been detained in Scotland by bad weather. "I've never had a baby before, and there are a thousand things that should have been done before this happened. With mother and Ellen both gone—"

She took the baby from his crib and laid him in Gary's arms.

"You are the first person besides me to hold Gerald Fulton Samuels," she said.

He held the child close to him, and looked down into its tiny, pinched face. He felt a wave of warmth and gentleness sweep through him, and he lifted the baby and held it close to his chest.

"I guess this makes everything complete for you, Holly," he said. "Nothing more can be added."

"It's almost a new life, Gary. Now, I shall never be alone again – not for a long time."

He was not sure what she had meant until five years later. Fulton was lecturing at a university in Switzerland when the child died suddenly. Gary saw the mask lifted from her then. She was unhappy in her grief, but her unhappiness went deeper than that. He knew that

Holly had never been loved. She had been respected, and treated with kindness and generosity, but she had needed to be loved, constantly and quietly loved, with patience, without the interference of Fulton's fame. The child's death made that need even greater. He had an aching desire to tell her how constant his love had been, how patient.

"You haven't been really happy, Holly."

He wondered if she suspected that his being near when she needed someone had not been accidental.

"I've never been extremely unhappy," she said, turning away from him.

"But you've been very lonely."

"Desperately," she said. "Even while traveling with Fulton, I've never had him with me alone. It's always been a crowded jump from one place to another. When Fulton is home, the house is flooded with people, intellectual people who expect me to be intellectual." She faced him squarely. "Gary, I'm not. I'm just a woman. I don't give a hoot for the walking brains who fawn on Lucy Valever's money. Sometimes I wish I were back in Jefferson Street."

It was not long after that he went to Europe. Nearly two years later, he met Fulton in Rome.

"I supposed you've heard that we're living in Holly's old house now," said Fulton, not with satisfaction. "Surrounded by rooming-houses and a multitude of noisy kids. Holly is still upset by the baby's death. It isn't right for a woman to grieve so long."

He saw Fulton many times afterward, and at each meeting, Fulton spoke more distastefully of the old house.

"I never thought Holly was one to crawl back into the past," he said. "She's becoming more and more difficult for me to reach."

And after he died, Gary thought that even in death Fulton Samuels should not be returned to Jefferson Street.

As he stood before the house now the sadness of the street vanished quietly upward into the shadows of the great elms, its age disappeared as he faced Holly's work of restoration.

He limped up the broad brick walk to the semi-circular steps. On either side, the variegated phlox were beginning to bloom, and beyond them, fresh balls of white were forming on the new hydrangeas. A bank of Keria at a corner of the porch held its small yellow blossoms daintily at the end of its branches. The air was warm and sweet. It was Holly's house again, and for an instant, Gary thought he heard the sound of an old horse's hoofs on the pavement. The illusion vanished when a boy, pounding the end of a stick against the sidewalk appeared across the street.

When Gary reached the porch, he paused before taking hold of the doorknocker. Suddenly, a pleasant excitement wept through him. During that instant he felt that all the self-discipline of his life had been shed and lay now at his feet. There were no more barriers between him and Holly. He felt it intensely, as if Holly had spoken the words herself. In a single moment, his entire life's journey culminated in his decision to stay on Jefferson Street.

"No," he said to himself. "Life can't change so abruptly."

But he knew it could. It had when he was seventeen, and it could again.

The End

The Scintilla

By Raymond Johnson

"Hah," Margolis scoffed. "Those big businesses ain't so easy. Mostly, they're like being in a big woods. Better a boy stays in a simple, quiet business like mine. "Hah? Don't fool yourself, Kid."

Not Bruno Franconi. Working for Margolis in his little store held no promise. Margolis was a good Jew, kept a good trade even though there was a supermarket across the street, but a boy of seventeen, crazy with ambition, couldn't get big just by chasing rats out of the storeroom or by cutting open packing cartons. The bigness of life, the greatness of men, lay outside, in the mills, the factories, the stockyards, in the railroads.

Margolis opened his cash register and took out some bills. He licked a fleck of raw hamburger from his thumb and counted Bruno's wages into his hand.

"You don't find another job; come back," he said. "I like you. You walk crooked, but you think straight. You come back to Margolis. Some day, you own a nice store."

"Sure," said Bruno with eagerness to be gone. "Thanks, Mr. Margolis. You're a good guy, but I want a job with opportunities for advancement, like at the steel mill."

"I know," said Margolis. "Big man."

Bruno limped to the door. "Goodbye, Mr. Margolis."

"So long, Kid. Don't forget what I said. Even big men get lost in the woods."

"Sure," said Bruno, and he went out upon the summer street.

He would miss the little store. It was full of rich, tangy smells and tastes, the smell of oranges stored in fragrant crates, making you thirsty every time you caught a whiff, the smell of cheese that went clear down to the stomach and agonized you until you went over the block and hacked off a flake. And he would miss the old man. Good-hearted Margolis, nice to kids, even to kids who painted "Margolis is a Jew bastard" across his windows on Halloween.

But Cripes, a boy with ambition, can't get anywhere in a place like Margolis's.

"Mr. Bruno Franconi, distinguished proprietor of Margolis's Market..." Now, that would look silly under your picture in a whisky ad. Mr. Waring, president of the steel mill, had his picture in the whisky ad once. Old man Waring had done all right. Started as an office boy. A guy can start that way, and if he's smart and full of vinegar, there's no telling how high he can go.

Bruno got off the streetcar in the part of town where he was born, near the mill on the bank of the river. When he was very small, he used to lie in bed and watch the mill labor under its own light. There was comfort in the presence of the sprawling giant. Being alone at night, only eight, with your mother out working, a boy's sort of scared, and he needs something big and light and noisy like the mill near him to make him feel safe. He used to watch with wonder and amazement the pink and green smoke come out of the stacks in masses thick as long clumps of colored cotton, and he went to sleep with the song of its clatter in his ears. The mill was a vulgar giant, waste matter pouring out of her into the river like an endless movement of stormy bowels, and cruel to men, now and then sending them out with cooked flesh or crushed bones. Yet to Bruno, the mill was a symbol of wealth and power, of strength he sometimes ached to possess.

"Mr. Bruno Franconi, distinguished steel mill executive…"

As he limped down the hill, he was filled with a profound sensation, as if his veins were pulsating with vitality. Such a feeling was never evoked by Mr. Margolis's store.

When he came upon the mill, it did not look the same as he remembered it. The buildings were the same, but the gray paint he remembered now was a thick coat of dirt and soot. There was activity and noise, but with them was a laborious effort. The scrap and coke piles he remembered as mountainous were only heaps now in his eyes. The giant mill seemed tired and sick.

Bruno approached the gate and presently sat within a glass cage before an old man who wore a gold pin in reward for his thirty years of service. Part of the mill's sickness was on the old man's face. The man grasped at words as he tried to tell Bruno that the mill had no place for cripples, and he stumbled like a cripple himself.

"You know how it is, son. Hazards and all that. Insurance companies—Too much of a risk, but we need good heads. It's a management policy, but we do need brains—Sometimes there've been exceptions, but management – I don't know—We need brains, that is."

The sickness clung.

He asked Bruno his name.

"Franconi – uh, huh. Italian, isn't it? We have a few Italians."

He looked up over his glasses, and the look talked to Bruno: Management, you know. Dagoes are a risk. Troublesome lot. I remember the bootleg days, then the black-market stuff, now the gambling rackets—numbers, the bookies, slots—and the labor rackets—Dagoes—

Bruno took his eyes from the face of the man.

When the old man left him alone for a minute, he felt like something in Margolis's meat case. People walked back and forth all the time outside the cage, tired, unhappy people, carrying papers and books, sometimes just walking, and they looked at him through the glass as if he were a green herring. He felt the sickness come over him.

He did not see what he had expected to find. There were no faces bright with ambition and hope, but frowning faces, pale ones, depressed, some too red, some the color of beef left overnight in water. Some of the faces smiled, but they were smiles masking hatred or jealousy. There was no brisk movement of vitality. There was haste, but it was sparked by shattered nerves, not energy. There was plodding. One man slunk along, suddenly becoming animated when an important-looking man passed through the room, and when he was gone, the slinker sat down in a chair and looked stupid.

Bruno quit looking. "I won't be like this," he thought. "It's what's in a guy that makes him sour. I've got the kind of stuff that won't sour."

The old man returned. He said there was a job typing work orders in the production department. Bruno said he had learned to type, and his hopes soared as he was led through the deafening noise, the intense heat and the suffocating smells of the factory toward an interview.

He came to a large room where twenty men and women sat at typewriters or at desks covered with prints and graphs and charts, each in his secret world of greatness. The room was disorderly. There was confusion and worry on the faces of the men and women, and fear. In this room, a thousand headaches a year were born.

At the front of the office was another glass-walled room where a man with fierce eyes and wild black hair was shouting into the telephone. The old man entered this room, spoke briefly to the fierce one's secretary, then left Bruno alone, walking away with his fingers caressing his thirty years.

Bruno felt weak and dried up in the presence of the violent character who howled the mill into a laborious movement. His stomach shook, as happened the night a drunk jumped out of an alley and grabbed him. He was more than ever aware of his crippled leg.

He thought of Margolis. "It ain't easy …Mostly, they're like being in a big woods…"

Mr. Waaring…the whisky ad…

A frail young clerk came to the door, and stood beside Bruno to await the fierce one's attention. He had a sickness on his face. He had come one day with a big vision of greatness, and now his mouth and his eyes told that the vision was dead, and his only greatness was in his mother's heart or maybe in his wife's hope. The papers in his white, skinny hand trembled a message of fear.

Bruno watched him go up to the animal who led him. His voice was weak, but he tried to talk as if he had courage. The animal took the papers from his hand, and the youth straightened himself, drew in his breath and waited. Maybe there would be a crumb of praise. The hope died when the fierce one opened his mouth and howled his authority, spitting his greatness and slobbering his gigantic degenerate ego into the youth's face.

Bruno felt the other's pain as he was flailed by abuse. His stomach shriveled, and his crippled leg seemed to have hot needles sticking in it. He waited for the pale, sick clerk to explode and let a million arrows of anger fly into the fierce one, but he only stood still, redfaced, crisp and dry, with guts of dust.

Bruno choked on the thickness of his tongue, and he left the young man to the fierceness of his superior.

As he started to leave the building, he glanced toward the old man who sat, tired, hopeless, within his glass bottle. He lifted his hand, waved feebly, then went out into the hot, cindered parking lot, away from the building. He turned and looked back. The old man was watching after him, watching him limp away, with a sick smile. He raised his hand, and suddenly Bruno felt sorry for him, terribly sorry for him and for the other people he had seen.

Upon returning to the store, the sight of Mr. Margolis puttering behind the meat counter brought Bruno some comfort. Margolis looked up and smiled. Bruno remained silent. He proceeded to the back room, retrieved his apron from its nail, and tied it around his waist.

Without looking at him, Margolis said, "You find a job at the steel mill?"

Bruno went behind the meat block and cut a flake of cheese. "Aw, that place down there is enough to make a guy cuss," he said.

The End

A Man Got to Defy

By Raymond Johnson

Joe Schedule, a physically enormous black man of forty-five, had a big love, but not a very good place to keep it.

His boy Homer, fourteen, who was studying the piano, and his daughter Lucy, almost a schoolteacher at seventeen, kept his big chest swollen with pride. His wife Birdie was getting ready to give him a new child, and she was the sweetest, gentlest creature that ever set a plate of fried shrimp before a hungry man. But the three-room unpainted shack he rented in a dilapidated street in N----r Town was no fit place to keep on crowding all the love and pride that never seemed to stop growing in him.

"When I was makin' sixty cents an hour, we fit it real snug," he told John Swenson during lunchtime. "But at a buck an' a half an hour, it's a mean rat hole."

Joe was a cupola-tender in a foundry. It isn't easy for a black man to get that high in a foundry, but Joe was good with iron, and he knew how to get along with the sort of white men who suck foul-founding air all day for a living. He was nigger to them, and they never let him forget it. But Joe didn't care, because he knew that not even a dollar and a half an hour would let him be anything else among white men.

"Ever try to get a place up by Grover's Park?" asked Johnny.

Johnny was a friend of Joe's. He was the only white in the plant who treated him like a man and not just a good nigger with a heavy heat of iron. They nearly always ate lunch together in a corner of one of the molding floors. It was Joe who alone had caught a smell of hell to save Johnny's life. A big ladle cracked one afternoon, and in scrambling to a safe spot, Johnny kicked the support of a four-hundred-pound wheel pattern, which fell and pinned him in the path of the flaming orange liquid the ladle poured. There wasn't time to check the crawling death with sand, and Joe walked through the stuff, lifting the weight from Johnny's terrified form, and carrying the man to safety, cradled in his long, powerful arms as if he were a baby.

"Nice houses up at Grover's Park," Johnny said.

Joe had tried Grover's Park. They were fine houses, he knew. High on a hill, with real bluegrass lawns, plenty of space for geranium beds and a dogwood tree. Cool in summer, with a sweetness in the air. And in the winter, your lungs didn't choke up with soot like they did down where Joe lived.

"But they are quality folks, Johnny," said Joe. "They frown on folks like me, the same as white folks frown on them. Ain't no difference atween us, 'cept my ears is full of foundry dirt an' I take a bath only when the tubs ain't full of wash. Them folks have they wash did out, but it don't matter because they have bathtubs. Man, if I had a honest-to-God bathtub, I'd take a bath ever' day."

Joe said Homer and Lucy wouldn't be happy up by Grover's Park. They would be only nigger kids up there till they had time to prove their talents, and that takes a long time anywhere.

But they's old 'nough to stan' up and defy," he said. "An' they would, too, because they know I got an earnin' for a nice house with an inside toilet an' floors that won't splinter my feet. That's what I'm aimin' to have, Johnny."

He almost had it once. An agent for property owners at Grover's Park invited him into his office to talk about a seven-room house with a bath and a half.

"And the price is only twenty-two thousand," the agent had said.

Figures like that made Joe's head buzz with the piercing staccato of the squeezer machines on the foundry floor.

"Say that again – slow," Joe had said. "My mind all of a sudden is twistin' and turnin'."

The agent reiterated the price. Joe smacked his lips, slapped his legs, and burst into a deep, hearty laugh.

"Man, you killin' me. I ask for a drink of water an' you turn the hose in my face."

He laughed at himself when he told Johnny about it. "But I was kind of sore when I found out the house sold for twelve thousand to a man who makes dishpans for a livin'. I know that ain't right, Johnny, but I can't stay sore. Got to keep my mind aimed at the right kind of place for my family."

Icky Koulaski, who had been eating lunch with his crew near a stack of flasks, had heard Joe talking.

"Whatsa matter, Joe?" he said. "Them nigger snobs crawlin' under your hide?"

Icky was a molding foreman. He was a brawny Pole with a knife-scarred face, and powerful muscles like knotted rope under the skin of his naked shoulders. "You niggers have a hell of a time."

Johnny Swenson worked for Icky and he didn't like him. Icky was tough, and he bullied his men. But the thing Johnny hated most was the way he called the blacks nigger. He didn't say nigger. It was "neeg-gerr." And he made the word sound filthy, drawing it out in a verbal sneer.

"Ain't you seen the bulletin board?" said lanky Bill McGuire, biting off half a banana. "Notice on the board about a house."

"I could look at the board, an' it wouldn't mean nothin'," said Joe. "I can't read my own name less I write it myself."

"Ah, that house ain't nothin'," said Icky, waving his arms toward Joe. "I know that place. Lousy an' dirty. Cecil Yokum, up in the office, owns it. Wouldn't spend a dime to keep it up; now he thinks some dumb punk'll pay a premium for it. Why should Joe buy a rat hole when he can rent one."

"What the hell?" said Bill McGuire. "Why boil over about a house long as you've got a roof over your head."

"It's more'n a roof I want," said Joe. "I want a yard with grass. I like to walk in my bare feet on grass wet with dew. I want a tree or two, an' tulips in the spring. I wants room for my kids to grow. I wants to be happy."

"You've got the right idea," said Johnny Swenson. He spat in a mound of black sand as if to emphasize what he said, as if to forestall anyone else's challenge to Joe's right to happiness.

"Me, I've grown enough," said Bill McGuire. "Give me a dame and' a bottle, an' I'll lay my head on a rock."

"I got a good friend who buys an' sells real estate," said Icky. "Name's Holly Nichols. He'd cheat his own brother, but he's square with anyone I send him. See Holly, Joe. He'll give you a good deal, an' I need a few bucks commission."

"Ok," said Joe. "I'll see anybody effen. I can get a room for my boy's Piana."

Icky slid off the barrel he had been perched on. "Still time for a quick beer. Let's go over to the Crystal Bar."

He and his men put on their shirts and went out, leaving Joe and Johnny together.

"That Icky." Said Johnny, lighting a cigarette. "I hate the way he thinks. He doesn't care whether you got a decent house. He's after a commission. That's all. I hate the way he calls you guys niggers."

Joe laughed. "Nobody cares, Johnny. I got a buck-and-a-half fever, and bein' nigger's got to go with that."

"Don't you hate it, Joe? Don't it make you mad?"

"Effen a man calls you a bastard, it don't make you mad because you know you ain't a bastard. I knows I'm a man, a big man. I takes up a lot of room an' I got to pay for it some way. A man like me got to take what he don't like. He got to defy by just bein' happy. I knows Icky's tongue'd make the name Jesus soun' bad."

Saturday, Joe went to see Holly Nichols. He was a short, round man whose belly slopped over his belt like a half-empty sack of flour. He wore a dirty brown felt hat on the back of his head, and he talked to Joe through stained teeth that clenched a dead cigar stub. His office was a shabby storeroom with a rolltop desk, two discarded dining-room chairs and a telephone. One wall of the room was papered with dusty flyspecked slicks of dilapidated houses, collapsing apartment buildings and portions of rundown farms. Nichols called Joe Mr. Skettle.

"I'll be on the level with you, Mr. Skettle," he said. "I got a reputation to protect, an' I wouldn't charge you one dime over a client's bottom price just so's I could pay that dirty Pole a few bucks commission."

Nichols informed Joe that he currently had no listing good enough. However, when he discovered that Joe had almost two thousand dollars saved up in a can at home, his enthusiasm propelled him out of his chair.

"You can bet your last buck on a moose race that I'll have what you want by next Saturday," he said. "Now, the fifteen hunert you have is chicken feed in these times. Two thousand will talk a lot louder, Mr. Skettle. Two thousand cash will make a seller think hard."

"They's a lot of difference," said Joe.

Nichols removed the cigar stub from his mouth and pursed his lips. He dug his thumbs into his vest pockets and rocked back and forth.

"I like you, Mr. Skettle," he said after a thoughtful moment. "Tell you what. I'll loan you five hunert, an' you can pay it back ten bucks a week at two percent on balance, Mr. Skettle. How's at?"

Joe wrinkled his forehead and scratched his cheek. He could figure out the heat of molten iron by looking at it, but things like percents that can't be seen only brought a whirling to his mind.

"Ain't much, is it?" he said.

Nichols cackled. "Why two percent of five hunert is only ten lousy bucks, Mr. Skettle."

"Sounds like a good square deal," said Joe, and the whirling in his mind stopped.

"One thing about this, Mr. Skettle," Nichols said in deep confidence. "The deal's got to be strictly our secret. Say nothin' to nobody. I don't have a lot of money, an' I can't afford to have a lot of people houndin' me for deals like ours. Unnerstan'? It's a secret deal, Mr. Skettle. Know what I mean?"

"I knows," said Joe, spreading his mouth in a wide grin. "I sure knows. The best things are kept secret till last. Like the presents, Sandy Claus brings kids at Christmas."

He kept his secret. He said nothing to Johnny, nothing to Birdie. He had intended to keep his house a secret from Birdie until the last delicious moment when she would have to sign the papers with him.

With his secret, he was happy all week. His heart was light, his mind was free, and he sang at his work despite the great heat of his furnace blasting all day at the asbestos front of his clothing. All he could see in the glare of his furnace as the iron ran out was Lucy happy at her learning, Homer practicing on his piano in the corner of a large living room. He was proud and happy, and even the cranes in the foundry sang as they carried their fiery cargo to their floors.

Joe heard nothing from Nichols, but he had no doubt that Saturday would bring him word. Nichols was a good man, and he had not betrayed his confidence.

During lunch hour on Friday, Johnny Swenson remarked, "That man sure better deliver tomorrow. If he disappoints you, you'll hit rock bottom, and we won't be able to dig you out."

Bill McGuire threw his lunch paper down at Johnny's feet. "You got a good house, Johnny. Let Joe move in with you."

Johnny's face reddened. He shrugged and did not answer.

Icky Koulaski was gulping milk from a bottle. He let it trickle from the corners of his mouth as he talked. "Neighbors'd kick the hell out of him."

"Hell with the neighbors," said Johnny.

"You'd think hell if you rented your house to niggers," said Icky. "When I was a kid, a guy down the street from us rented to niggers, and man, what a riot."

Joe looked at Johnny. White patches of anger formed about his mouth as he stared at Icky.

"Jeez, what fun," roared Icky. "Whole neighborhood exploded. Swarmed on that house like crazy bees. Burnt the house down with them niggers in it, only they got away. Jeez." He roared again and slapped his legs. "Bet them niggers is still runnin'."

"Where in hell were the cops?" said Johnny.

"Cops!" Icky yelled. "Whoever seen cops at a nigger fight."

The whistle blew to call the men back to work. Johnny glared at Icky's broad, dirty back. He picked up a small wooden flat and started to throw it at the mass of contemptible flesh.

"Dirty sonofa—"

Joe clutched his arm.

"There's a lot of arn to get up, Johnny. It needs all the heat we got."

He went back to his furnace, but his afternoon work was harder than the chores of the morning had been. He tried not to think about anything but Saturday, but Johnny's wrath stayed in his mind.

"Why does the boy get all fired up about me?" he asked himself. He was afraid for Johnny.

Saturday, Nichols called him and told him to bring his can to the office. Everything about the foundry slid out of his mind.

Nichols was affable. His eyes gleamed like a ferret's when Joe showed him the can.

"Looks like we're goin' to do business," he said. He pushed a picture across his desk. "Take a look at your new house, Mr. Skettle."

Joe's eyes bugged out as he admired the picture. He shook his head and smacked his lips.

"Sweet, ain't it," said Nichols. "All white, story an' a half, five rooms an' a bath."

"But us is colored folks," said Joe. "Ain't no house like that for colored folks."

Nichols chuckled. "Hard to believe, ain't it, Mr. Skettle. Too sweet to be true." He stood up, leaned over Joe's shoulder and pointed a nailless index finger at the picture. "Loot at that gorgeous picket fence. Them twigs hangin' on it is roses—climbin' roses. In the spring, they bloom like wild."

"Almost smell the breeze already," said Joe.

"Yeah," laughed Nichols. "Has a swell lot, too. All grass—thirty-five by fifty."

"Them numbers on the steps—plain as day," said Joe.

"The address," said Nichols, "Smart Avena, 1832 South. Owned by a old lady an' her daughter. They're asking' ten thousand."

Joe gasped. His mouth hung open.

"But I can squeeze 'em a little," Nichols added hastily. "They need the dough to swing a deal down south. Got to do somethin' this week. How's seventy-five hunert?"

Joe closed his mouth. "At's better." He studied the picture for a moment, and frowned.

"I been thinking," he said. "Smart avena—is that colored folks?"

"Don't you read the papers?" said Nichols. "Smart Avena all the way to Twentieth is changin' over to colored people."

"My boy didn't read me nothin' like that," said Joe.

"It's right," said Nichols. "Don't let it worry you none. Ain't no law separatin' folks anyhow."

"My boy read me that," said Joe. "Ain't no law says some folks is black an' some is white—but that's the way it is, an' that's the way it is."

It was a confusing business, this buying a house. His head couldn't handle it. With time ticking away and a barrage of terms like mortgages, deeds, titles, insurance, taxes, and collateral swirling around him, Joe could only muster a bemused "Whoo-ee!"

He looked at the house on Sunday, and Monday evening, he gave Mr. Nichols a note for five hundred dollars. The next evening, Mr. Nichols had possession of his can. Wednesday morning, Icky Koulaski confronted him.

"Didn't I see you on Smart Avena Sunday?"

Joe gave him a broad grin and nodded.

"I wasn't sure," said Icky, and his mouth turned down at the corners. "I took my time to make sure."

The noise from the sand mixer, and the clamor from the cleaning-room came between them.

Joe's grin dropped from his face. "You said somethin' then like you was mad."

"You ain't bought a house lately?" said Icky.

Joe figured out the heat of the iron in Icky's eyes. The sweat on his forehead was not from his labors. He nodded.

"Smart avena?" said Icky,

Now Joe saw the iron was hideous hate.

"That's my street, Joe. You was in my block."

All the noises of the foundry struck Joe's ears at once. The roar of the fire guns, the chatter of the roll-overs, the throb of the sand lifts, the dry-bone rattle of massive chain links, the angry spitting of a broken air hose—all made silent Icky's next words. But Joe saw them on his lips.

"Change your mind, Joe."

Joe felt the coldness of fear. It was not physical fear of Icky, but the fear that a great, horrible blunder of his had upset the peace of the foundry.

In the brief silence that came, Icky's loud voice attracted the attention of the naked-chested men working nearby.

"You ain't buyin' a house on Smart avena, Joe. I an' a lot of other guys here own houses up there. We ain't about to let no niggers make dumps out of 'em." He wiped a trickle of sweat from his chest with a dirty thumb and walked away.

Joe felt weak as he watched him go. For a moment, he could only stand and stare at the great furnace being made ready for its charge. He had a strong urge to go to the timekeeper and check out, but it submitted to the violent wave of anger that swept through him.

"Homer—Lucy—God knows an' us knows he is black. But us can't be ashamed because ever'body else is."

Then he worked like a driven slave, bursting with a thirstless, hungerless, gigantic energy.

He hated the lunchtime whistle when it blew. The days of congenial gathering of Icky's crew seemed long in the past. Now, every white face he saw out of the corner of his eye had a sickness on it. He could have taken the dare he saw in the eyes of every man in Icky's crew, but it wasn't in his heart to defy that way. He liked to smile at a white man's face and get a smile in return.

He passed Johnny Swenson, sitting alone. Johnny stopped him.

"If you're headin' for the cleanin' room, think again," said Johnny. "Those blacks in there are sore."

"What for?" said Joe.

"They know what's goin' on, an' they don't like it. You never eat lunch with them, an' if you go in now, they'll think you're scared yellow."

Joe sat down and held his face in his hands. "What have I done, Johnny? What have I done? I set the world on far."

"It ain't that bad," said Johnny, peeling a banana.

"I wants to buy peace and happiness an' what I makes is trouble."

"That damned Koulaski!" said Johnny. "Another day of poison drippin' out of his mouth, an' everybody in the plant will be knifin' each other."

"Icky'd crow the rest of his life about how he showed the big n----r who was boss," said Johnny. "The other blacks here don't want to think you're yellow, Joe."

"They don't matter none," said Joe.

"What about Homer an' Luey? You goin' to kick them in the teeth?"

Johnny, I don't want no trouble. I don't want to fight Icky or any other man."

"No, I know," said Johnny. "I never wanted to fight either. I always thought things worked themselves out, but I guess I never had anything to fight about. I never went where there were any Icky Koulaskis."

Joe returned to work, feeling drained and with the realization that the day was only halfway through.

The next morning, Icky came up to him with four other men. They were surly. Joe smiled, but their faces were like sand rammed into a mold of hate. Icky himself had a bulldog look, and he stood with his legs apart, his arms folded across his naked chest.

"Changed your mind yet, Joe?" He said. "Us Smart Avena people got to know."

Joe wanted to say yes and have peace again. But he knew there would be no peace. When he thought of giving in, his mind pictured Homer at the piano and, Lucy filling a blackboard with writing, the black men at the plant leaning on him.

"My mind's too twisted," he said.

"Then untwist it," Icky said. "We want to know by tomorrow. An' keep your big mouth shut. You've got the niggers so stirred up they won't do no work."

Joe faced him squarely. "That ain't the truth. I ain't said nothin' to nobody."

Icky took a few steps toward him. His thick, muscular arms dropped to his sides. His head came down; his chest swelled up.

"I don't like nobody callin' me a liar."

"I ain't called you a liar, Icky—"

"Mr. Koulaski." Icky spat the words out. "Mis-ter Koulaski."

Johnny Swenson had stepped over from his machine. The corners of his lips quivered with anger. He stood to one side of Joe.

"Why don't you let this man alone?"

Icky turned, took a few steps toward him, and stood with his hands on his hips.

Johnny said, "You're only tryin' to get Joe to start trouble so the boss'll be on his neck."

"Listen, you nigger-lovin' little Swede," Icky snarled, "keep your nose out of my business or get big enough to back up your talk."

He walked away, and the other men followed him.

The next day was payday. No one approached Joe all morning. No word was spoken to him. He saw that everyone was watching Icky, as if for some sort of signal. Maybe Icky had a scheme. It was easy to get hurt in a foundry. He had seen men cooked in the fiery orange juice. No matter how it happened, it always could be made to look like an accident.

Joe worked hard, trying to squeeze the cold from his fingertips, fighting the horrible nervousness in his belly. When the noon whistle blew, he felt great relief. He almost ran as he went toward the superintendent's office.

Johnny Swenson stopped him.

"I'm goin' for my check," Joe said.

"I can't stop you, Joe," said Johnny. "But I'm goin' with you. The boss has got to know why you're runnin' out."

"Stay away, Johnny," said Joe. "Let me go, an' this'll be all over. I'm scared, but not for my skin only. If I stays, this plant's goin' to be one big nigger fight."

Johnny went with him to the superintendent's office, and, in angry words, gave the boss the story of the brewing fight. Joe was sent back to his job. Johnny was with him when Icky came out of the superintendent's office an hour later. Icky approached them like a bull that had been tormented in the ring. His scars were violet with rage.

"Yellowbellies!" All the flesh of his naked chest, shoulders and back seemed to quiver. "The boss docked me the afternoon to do some thinkin'. I've already done it. I dare you to walk up Smart Avena after today, Joe. The committee'll be pokin' sand down the boss's throat for this Monday."

When he was gone, Joe said, "This ain't good. I told the boss it wouldn't be no good."

Johnny could see that. He made no answer.

Joe ran off his afternoon heat clumsily. He poured dirty iron, and spilled it. He didn't see iron all afternoon, only Birdie. He hated his secret. He wished he had told Birdie what he had done, what a sickness he had brought on himself.

"Birdie'd a knowed I shouldn't a did it."

He longed for her comforting touch to soothe his throbbing head. She possessed the skill to calm a man's troubled mind. She had made him happy during their poor days. That happiness had gone during their prosperity. Tonight, he would go home from the plant for the last time, tell her how his ignorant head and black face had brought evil to their house, and she would return peace to his mind.

At quitting time, he gave the other men ten minutes lead so they would be away from the Crystal Bar when he went in to get his check cashed. He wanted to see no more of the foundry men that day or ever. He would work in sewer mud in ditches again. Right now, all he wanted was to talk to Birdie.

The thought of her was making things peaceful already. The day was over. Icky and the other men would be forgotten tomorrow. The squeezing at his temples had relaxed. Things didn't seem so bad.

As he walked to the Crystal Bar, his steps were long, and quick with spirit. The fatigue he had carried all day was gone. His muscles were singing. Home and Birdie. They could be happy in a shabby, unpainted shack. Niggers knew how. They could make the dirt-fogged air seem sweet. They could make grimy houses seem bright in the pale evening sun.

Nearing the bar, he saw Johnny Swenson. Johnny was a good-looking boy in his street clothes, his face washed clean. He would miss Johnny. Johnny was a good friend.

"You goin" in there, Joe?" said Johnny, indicating the bar.

Joe nodded.

"Icky's in there."

Joe looked up at the dirty face of the building.

"Guess he's waitin' for me."

"All of Smart Avena seems to be with him," said Johnny. "Icky called me a dirty name, but I let on like I didn't hear. I wouldn't go in if I was you, Joe."

Joe's big lips were dry, his eyes huge.

"Guess I got to now, Johnny."

He moved a few steps toward the door, paused and considered, as if trying to see inside the men he would face.

"I been thinkin' a lot about Birdie an' Homer an' Lucy. What I done ain't wrong. I can't raise my kids to stan' up an' defy less I do it myself."

Johnny looked at him intently.

"I'm goin' in, too, Joe."

"Ain't no good, Johnny. I ain't at the foundry now, an' what happens can happen just to me. Stay here, Johnny. Promise."

Joe went through the door. He paused inside. In a moment, Johnny was beside him.

A dozen men were at the bar. None turned. Others were scattered at tables and in the booths. Their voices were high, and no lull followed the door's closing. The jukebox was shrieking to the left. The room was filled with smoke, the smell of beer and boiled shrimp. Shapeless, moving shadows were cast by garish blinking neon tubes behind the bar.

Johnny stayed close behind Joe. He stared at the booth where Icky Koulaski was sitting.

Joe swallowed a hard, dry fear in his throat. He walked slowly toward the bar, toward the end where the cash register stood. The bartender finished drawing a beer, and then approached Joe, wiping his hands on his apron. He took Joe's check, opened the cash register, and counted money into Joe's hand.

The jukebox nickels' worth died. The voices droned on, diminished, and then there was quiet.

Icky Koulaski was standing up, facing Joe. The scars on his face were like streaks of fire through the stubbly brush on his beard.

"There's the nigger thinks he's movin' up on Smart Avena" his voice was like a small cannon in the room.

All eyes in the room shifted towards Joe. The men at the bar initially glanced at Icky before redirecting their attention to Joe. The bartender observed Joe's expression with concern. Unperturbed, Joe focused solely on counting his money, paying no heed to the glances exchanged around him.

Johnny Swenson came up to his side.

"Ready, Joe," he said.

"When I counts my money," said Joe.

Icky came toward him. He had been drinking, but he was steady on his feet. The other men knotted together in the center of the room. The men at the bar pocketed their change and got to their feet. Two of them hurriedly left the barroom.

"Come on, Joe," said Johnny.

Joe turned from the bar, his money still in the palm of his hand.

"Buyin any houses today?" Icky sneered. He flung his hand out against Joe's, scattering the money in every direction.

Joe backed up against the bar. His eyes drilled into Icky's ugly face. His dry, thick lips parted only a little.

"Icky," he said quietly, "you oughtn't a did that."

Johnny Swenson stepped over to Icky. "Leave us alone," he said hotly. "If you know what's good for you, get back to your booth and shut up."

"Hear that?" Icky said, turning to his men. "This nigger-lovin' punk's threatenin' me." He turned suddenly and grabbed Johnny's shirt.

Johnny jerked free, and flung an arm up into Icky's face. Icky smashed a hard fist into his chin.

Joe straightened up, his huge shoulders rising, his back stiffening as muscles tensed. His head was big, black anger.

"Don't you hurt Johnny," he shouted. His arms drew parallel, his fists knotted together. Like a double ramrod, his arms drew parallel, his fists knotted together. Like a double ramrod, his arms shot forward, and his two massive, knuckled fists crashed against Icky's face.

Icky flopped against a table, his arms spread wide. He remained against the table for a few seconds, shook the thunder from his head and glared murderously at Joe.

Joe looked at his fists, then at Icky. "I'm sorry effen I hurts you," he said. "But I ain't foolin' to have Johnny hurt. You can beat me an' call me any names you want. That don't hurt none. But when you picks on my kids or my friends, I gets a powerful mad hurt inside."

He tugged at Johnny's arm. "Go on home, Johnny. Icky ain't botherin' nobody no more."

A beer bottle flung by Icky hit him in the back of the head, deflected and shattered the bubbly glass of the jukebox. Joe stumbled forward, stunned.

Johnny dived toward Icky, and let loose a rapid flow of hot fists against his hard belly. Joe swung around, and went in to pull him away. Icky, his face red with the pain of Johnny's unexpected power, shouted to the men around him.

"All right, you bums! What the hell I been drillin' you for?"

Four men clambered over chairs and landed on Joe. Icky caught one of Johnny's arms, and twisted it behind him. He lifted Johnny off the floor, pushed his head against the bar, and slammed a fist against his nose. Leaving Johnny, he turned to help the four who had proved no match for Joe.

Johnny snapped out of Joe's anesthesia, grabbed a bottle of whisky, flung it at Icky and missed. Two other men from the back of the room lunged at Johnny. He stepped aside; they crashed against the bar.

The bartender was busy clearing glassware from the back bar. A bottle aimed at Joe's head missed its mark, smashed into rows of highball glasses and sent millions of sparkling splinters through the air.

Joe was down on his knees. His arms were around the legs of two men who were beating his face and head. Icky was kicking him in the ribs when Johnny rushed in and flung himself upon his back. Joe got to his feet, his arms still wrapped around the men's legs. He whirled round and round, then flung the men away from him. One landed upon a table, the other on a chair, shattering it.

Bottles were flying again. The bartender sank to his knees and crawled toward the phone booth in the rear of the room.

Icky was back at Joe. He landed a nasty blow under Joe's heart. Joe fell to the floor, Icky throwing his full weight on top of him. One of the men who had suffered Joe's punishment picked up a chair leg and began beating on Joe's head.

Johnny jumped furiously on the man's back, clutching him by the throat. He was pulled off. He swung a terrific right to the jaw of his new assailant. The man went down but got up right away. In his hand was the bottom half of a beer bottle, the jagged edges up. Johnny couldn't help Joe anymore. The crazy man in front of him would require all his cunning. The man came toward him slowly, bleeding, his gritted-teeth mouth spread in an insane smile. Johnny braced himself, keeping his eyes on the ragged glass in the man's hand. The man closed in. Johnny's guard failed him.

Joe heard hideous screams. He thought they were his, but he couldn't tell. The relentless pounding on his head, hands, and face blurred his senses, rendering everything around him distorted and distant. Lost in the maelstrom, he struggled to recall the reason behind the surrounding frenzy.

Then he thought of Johnny, and in the brief flash of light that pierced the blood of his brain before he lost consciousness, he knew the screams were Johnny's. He struggled to get up and couldn't. He raised his bleeding hands above him.

"All right, all right," he cried, then began choking on his own blood. There was no house on Smart avena. He wanted to tell Icky.

He wanted to tell Birdie. But suddenly, everything got so quiet, and there was no one to tell anything.

When he woke up, someone was trying to move him. He howled with pain.

"Just want to get at these cuts," a husky voice said. It was a new voice, and it was clean, without hate.

Someone began washing his face gently with a cool, wet cloth.

He tried to open his swollen eyes. Only a slit let light through. He saw a cop kneeling beside him, holding a wet bloody towel.

Where's Johnny?" He tried to say, but he couldn't make the cop understand him.

Another cop was standing beside him, questioning the bartender. The bartender talked nervously, uneasily, scared of incriminating himself.

"I don't know who the men was. Half a dozen of 'em. Never seen 'em before. This guy—this'n on the floor—he come in, see—I wasn't payin' no attention—tending bar I don't hear every little thing, see—then all of a sudden this guy—this'n on the floor—then he pokes the big guy in the face—the white guy, that is—"

Joe raised a hand feebly. It took all his effort to make words come out of his mouth. "That ain't the truth. That ain't the truth. Ask Johnny. Johnny knows the truth."

There was a brief silence, then the cop standing up said to the bartender, "Who's Johnny?"

"The little guy," said the bartender. "He's the guy they just hauled away."

"Oh," said the cop. "Well, he can't talk." Then he said, not the bartender, not to anyone. "That damned bottle."

The End

The Tattered Sparrow

By Raymond Johnson

It was the best news Father Francis had brought to the river shanty for a long time. Bruno waited to hear no more. There was a ball of excitement inside him, and he wanted to make a noise, a loud noise, explode the ball, but if he did that, his mother would know he had been listening. He had to get outside, and if he didn't have a sloppy leg, he'd run over to the shack where Lee Monroe lived.

Lee would be eager to hear the good news. Lee would be pleased, nearly as pleased as Bruno Franconi, to know that the old man was in jail – maybe forever this time. Heck no, that would be too good a thing. Six months or a year at most. But what wonderful months. Day after day, through the whole winter, without a kick in the pants or a knot on the head, without watching his old man slam his mother around or kick Lee in the rump like he was a black dog instead of a boy. Six months of days without dread, nights without fear, without hatred.

Golly, it was so good he just had to get out and holler about it.

He slipped from his hiding place behind the partition, lifting his twisted foot, step by step, and carefully setting it down again so his mother would not hear it scrape over the rough boards of the kitchen floor. Once outside, the boy's body of impulse and impetuousness massed its energy for a long shout across the hundred yards of flat riverbank to the unpainted Monroe shack.

Then he saw Old Rotgut, his father's yellow cat, slinking toward a pile of cinders and tin cans, a froth of feathers hiding his greedy jaws. Bruno's shout of elation was cheated by a howl of rage at the cat. You may as well shout at the moon as at a cat.

Bruno picked up the stone at his feet and flung it without aim. Luck struck it painfully against Old Rotgut's spine. The cat dropped the sparrow to spit and snarl at its unseen foe, then dashed under the rotten porch of the house.

"Coward yellow bastard!" Bruno shouted after it.

He crossed the barren yard, cracked by Autumn drought and dead of the poisons of the factory-polluted river valley, and as he looked down at the tattered sparrow, a soft joy replaced his rage, for the bird was still alive. He picked it up and held it in his cupped hands, blowing his breath gently upon its head.

One wing was torn from its mooring, and blood bulbed into a small ruby set in a fractured joint. A red streak ran in a straight line from the injured wing, in violent contrast to the soft, dust-covered coat to the twisted, broken feathers of the tail.

The sparrow looked up into the boy's face with one terror-filled eye that glistened like a small brown bead. Bruno knew the horror and fear that sparked the glow of the eye, and his hatred for old Rotgut and for his father flamed again. It would be a wonderful thing, a wonderful thing if this bird could live.

Bruno put the sparrow in a matchbox and hid it away in the damp, moldy darkness under the icebox. Next, he would go over to

Lee's house and get some of the stuff Lee's Ma cooked up. She boiled roots for medicine, some for healing broken bones, some for fevers, and some were good for rat bites. Daisy Monroe had roots for everything that got wrong with people, and maybe there was something that would help heal a sparrow.

He said nothing to his mother and slipped quietly out of the house again. She would want the sparrow to live, but she would say the root boilings wouldn't do any good, not Daisy's root boilings.

Mom didn't like Daisy Monroe. She was a nigger, but that wasn't why. He liked Daisy, and Lee was the only friend he had. Lee was a swell runner, and he could climb trees like a squirrel. Lee got around faster, and he always found the most junk, but when they got paid, he always divvied up even. Funny Mom liked Lee so well and not his old lady. Maybe Mom would like her better if she had a husband. Daisy had two kids younger than Lee, and this seemed sort of queer because he couldn't remember ever seeing a father at Daisy's house. Heck, it must have been wonderful, with no old man around to beat on your head and kick you in the slats.

Maybe it would have been better for Lee yesterday if there had been a father in the place. His old man might have thought twice before he kicked the daylights out of Lee and chased him home.

He and Lee were on the floor counting the money they got from the junker Jew down by the steel mill for the sack of scrap iron they had collected. Lee had taken a sack of bottles, too, and they were trying to figure out if the junker man had paid for them. Bruno's mom was out on a job of washing, but even if she had been home she couldn't have saved Lee from the beating. She was little and scared, and the old man would have beaten her, too.

Bruno had seen the old man staggering toward the house, but it was too late to warn Lee or to scramble himself. When the old man saw Lee, he yelled black names and acted like the tornado that tore through the river valley in the spring.

"Get that black sonofabitch out of here," he hollered.

Lee's eyes widened in fear, making them as big as baseballs, and he was so terrified that he couldn't find the door. He crawled frantically in circles, as fast as his hands and knees could move, searching for something to hide behind. Meanwhile, the old man's big foot kept kicking him in the butt every inch of the way. Every time Lee sprawled, the foot cracked down on his back, and it made a noise like pounding on a hollow log. Lee howled and wailed, and Bruno could only sit on his twisted leg behind the stove and howl with him. Lee finally got to his feet, then the old man grabbed him and beat him on the head, and Lee screamed bloody murder. When Lee kicked the old man between the legs, the old man got madder than ever, but he was so busy holding himself and groaning he couldn't move. Lee found the door and was gone like a scared rabbit. Bruno scrambled out the door and hid in the hut of the dump-tender at the steel mill until the old man got sober enough to go out for another load.

"He can beat on himself in jail now," he said as he reached Lee's house. "It's a good thing, a good thing."

The door to Daisy's shack was tied shut with a rope, which meant Daisy was away on a job, and the kids had to stay in. Lucy Bee, the youngest, almost drowned in the river one day while Daisy was gone, and ever since then, Daisy tied her house up tight.

"Hey, Lee, in there?" Bruno shouted. "Hey, Lee."

There was no shout in answer, and Bruno loosened the knot of the rope. He went into the windowless room of the shack, and a little voice from the corner said, "I Luty Bee."

"Lo, Lucy Bee. Where's Lee?"

"Tick," said Lucy Bee.

"Lee got a mizry for sure," said Birdie Dee, holding Lucy Bee wrapped in a blanket.

The room was cold, and damp from the wash hanging on a line stretched from one wall to the other, and heavy was the smell of cooked lye and fat from homemade soap. Bruno ducked under the torn seat of Lee's overalls and saw Lee lying on a pallet of old blankets in front of the rusty wood-burning stove.

Bruno went over and got down on his knees beside him.

"What's the matter, Lee?"

Lee looked up at him but said nothing.

Bruno saw the beads of sweat on Lee's forehead and upper lip, like little sunburn blisters. Funny how oily nigger skin seemed when there was sweat on it.

"You hot, Lee?"

There was no answer. The thin blanket covering Lee had spasms, reminding Bruno of the tick in the corner of his old man's mouth.

"You mad, Lee?"

"Um, always cheated. Eva, time that junker man sees me, he knows he goin cheat me."

"Heck, Lee, we'll find some more bottles. We'll take a whole day, and we'll find some more bottles. We'll take a whole day, an we'll find so many bottles we'll have plenty of money even if we are cheated."

Lee turned his face away and looked up at the dilapidated stove.

"You know what, Lee? My old man's in jail."

Bruno was disappointed because Lee didn't seem to care.

"Ain't that swell? Now you can come over to my house all the time, and won't have to be scared of having your teeth kicked out."

"Um, always cheated," Lee said.

"Aw, I won't let you be cheated anymore. I'll stay right by you and do your countin'. Now, ain't it swell my old man's in jail?"

"Um, a black bastard."

"Oh, my old man talks like that all the time. Everything's a bastard or a sonofabitch to him."

"Um, a black bastard everywhere. I ain't a boy. Um, a black bastard. I get spit at an' cheated an' beat up on like a black bastard."

Lee kept on talking like that for a long time, just looked at the stove and talked to it like no one else was there in the room. He closed his eyes and lay quiet, then all of a sudden, he squeezed his face up like a prune, gritted his teeth and grabbed at his middle. He pulled his knees up to his stomach and groaned.

Bruno watched the pain twist the muscles of the oily face, then relax its hold. He was used to pain, the feel of it in his own body, the sight of it in his mother's face, but it was pain he understood. This that twisted Lee's face gave him a feeling in his stomach like he had when he was alone at night and heard noises that didn't belong to what he knew.

"I'm not afraid," he said to himself as he watched Lee. But he thought there must be something he should do to help Lee. Simply sitting around and watching wasn't enough. He recalled the sparrow trapped in the dark space beneath the icebox. He pitied the bird; it didn't belong there, but he had to hide it to keep it safe from Old Rotgut.

He wanted to tell Lee about the sparrow, and he waited for Lee to open his eyes. But Lee only lay quiet.

Bruno went over in the corner with Lucy Bee and Birdie Dee. Birdie Dee was putting some soap beads on a string. Lucy Bee was chewing on some of the beads, and her chin was wet with sudsy slobber. Bruno strung some beads and made a coronet for Birdie Dee. Soap beads were better than glass ones because you didn't have to unstring them. You just squashed them and pulled them off the string; then you rolled them into beads again.

He kept thinking about the sparrow. He ought to go home and see how it was. He wanted it to live, but he wasn't doing anything to help it live. He ought to go, but he didn't want to leave Lee.

"When did Lee get sick?" he asked Birdie Dee.

"He was sick all night. He bruised up like a truck hit him. Ma bloated um with root water."

Lee began moaning again, and Bruno scooted across the floor to his side. Lee looked real queer. He was straightened out still, and the oily skin was dry now. And when he opened his eyes, there were red streaks in them, and they stared up at the ceiling. Bruno thought the feeling in his stomach was worse.

"Lee, you all right?"

Lee moved his mouth, but he didn't say anything.

"Say, Lee, I got a sparrow at home. Saved it from Old Rotgut."

It wasn't like Lee not to care about things that were so important. Any other time, he would have been tickled to death to know Bruno's old man was in jail and that there was a sparrow where he could hold it and look at it any time he wanted to.

"Want me to go get it?"

Lee just went on staring.

"If I can have some of your ma's root water, I can get my sparrow well and maybe we can learn it to do tricks."

Lee pulled a hand from beneath his covers and whirled it in the air.

"UM a sparra. Can't learn a sparra nothin.' Sparras ain't good for nothin' but old mangey cats an' peckin' at the groun'."

"You can learn a pigeon."

"Um, a sparra," said Lee. Then he got the shivers so bad the old boards in the floor shook.

Bruno felt his stomach shake, too, worse than it ever had before. He wanted to get out of the cold, wet shack, and get away from Lee. He struggled to his feet.

"I'll go get my bird. You'll like him, Lee."

Lee looked at him then, and his eyes weren't so hard and empty.

"Don' go 'way."

"I've got to, Lee. I don't want my sparrow to starve to death."

"Don' lea' me," said Lee. "Don' lea Lucy Bee an' Birdie Dee."

"I've got to feed my sparrow. I'll be back."

He went outside and closed the door, looping the rope around a nail to hold it shut. The new wind coming down from the north, carrying the smell of sludge and sour gas from the refinery, was good on his face, and as he pulled his weight toward his own house, he noticed the feeling was gone from his stomach.

Well, he was just plain scared, that's all. Not of Lee, but of what was wrong with him, scared, in a mixed-up sort of way. Lee was lying there so funny, talking about being cheated all the time, about being a black bastard and a sparrow. Why, Lee never did care about being a nigger. Why should he? He could run, he could hunt, and he was a crackerjack with a slingshot, and in the wintertime, he had more fun sliding down a hill in a battered dishpan than most kids have on a sled. Why should he care if he was a nigger?

Maybe Lee was scared, too. He certainly seemed frightened, his eyes wide and staring, as if he had forgotten something crucial or had been told to stop searching for something lost because it was never his to find. Lee was mixed up.

Bruno went into the kitchen of his house. Mom was gone, either on a job of wash or to see his old man in jail. He got down on the floor and pulled the matchbox from under the icebox. The sparrow was still alive. The blood in the wing had stopped flowing; the ruby set had become a round maroon crust. The single eye still glowed up at him, unblinking, and like a brown bead, had no depth. Bruno lifted the box closer to him and blew gently upon the ragged feathers of the injured wing.

It must be near time for supper. He had worried about what to feed a sick bird. Seeds and bugs, but this was November, and where do sparrows look in November for seeds and bugs enough to keep alive? Bread. He found a wadded bread wrapper with some crumbs in it, and these he poured into the box. The sparrow ignored them.

Bruno thought about Lee and wondered if he had eaten all day, Lee, and the girls. Maybe he ought to go back and fix them some supper. He could find something in the up-ended orange crate Daisy used for pantry shelves. Lee was his friend, and he ought to take care of him. But he got that gosh-awful feeling every time he thought of Lee. Just squatting and looking at the sparrow he was all right, but thinking about Lee jumbled his insides.

He pushed the matchbox under the icebox again and went outside. He looked through the dead gray of river valley evening toward Lee's shanty. It looked dark and mysterious and sort of mad, as though hating to be shoved down in a shadowed hole. Lee was there, scared and mixed up and sick. He wished Mom was home so she could help him think what to do. Maybe he'd better go try to find her before he went to Lee's, but gosh, that would take forever.

The wind moaned through the power wires strung toward the steel mill. It reminded him of Old Rotgut, and he wished the cat would come sneaking out of hiding so he could throw another rock at it. Now, with the old man in jail maybe the cat would go away and stay forever. That would be a good thing. If Old Rotgut hadn't come along and cheated it, his sparrow would be pecking at the ground somewhere.

He went back into the house but didn't stop at the icebox. He knew he ought to go back to Lee, but Lee's sickness and the coming darkness made him more scared than ever. He went into the other room, slowly, looking into every darkening corner before he took a dragging step.

The room seemed a hundred times colder than it ever had before, filled with gloom and fear. The stiff brown wallpaper was soot and filled with the smell of rot and mildew. The rusty heating stove in the corner was not warm and friendly; it was only something to hide behind during the recklessness of his father's drunken storms.

He closed his eyes but did not sleep. He lay for a long time thinking about Lee and trying to recapture the joy he had felt when Father Francis brought the news about his father. It had gone, every particle of it. It was so long ago. Time is so long; everything that happens in the day is so old by night. He listened to the sounds of the darkness, the mouse in the kitchen, the low moan of the wind in the wires.

Then, there was another sound, a faint one from the distance, strange and fearful. He held his breath and waited. It came again, louder but muffled by the wind. It was a shriek, a cry, a moan, a prayer, all combined to form a wail of sorrow.

Bruno got up and stumbled through the door. The jumbled feeling in his stomach had become a powerful movement. He looked toward Lee's house, but he saw nothing but empty night, and he heard no more. The powerful physical movement remained inside him.

He went back into the kitchen and reached under the icebox. His fingers dipped gently into the matchbox to feel the tattered sparrow, but all they touched was a single feather, the mangled head and some bread crumbs.

The End

A Bum in Love

Raymond Johnson

Bart McBride was a bum.

When his mother died thirty years ago, he bought his first pair of crutches so he could go to her funeral without scooting on his rump, oared by his skinny arms. He had more confidence in those crutches than most people have in good legs. When he was well-soused, he would go to sleep hanging on them, his two hundred and twenty pounds of torso, shoulders and head balanced in deep slumber on his armpits.

With legs or without them, a kid doesn't grow up on Ninth Street unless he's tough. Bart had a soft streak that ran deep, rooted in the memory of his mother. When he found out the one-eyed preacher at the Apostolic Faith Mission had a gnawing desire for a glass eye, he dragged himself up and down Ninth Street for two winter weeks to collect enough money for the phony peeper.

Out of Bart's good streak, he had grown his hatred for Doc Prichard, who ran a dirty drug store at Ninth and Curvesy. He took Doc's whisky, slept in his store, and ate the food Doc's fountain boy, Harry, gave him, but he hated Doc with all the heart his big chest held. Doc was a good photographer, and in the basement of his store, he had a studio. The superimposed pictures he made sold for two bucks a piece in the washrooms of hotels and nightclubs and over confectionary counters near high schools.

When Bart killed Doc, Steve Perkins was the nearest thing to a relative he had to stick up for him. Steve was a night clerk at the Ajax hotel, across the street from Doc's store, and Bart's ticket in his cash box was over twenty-seven dollars. At eighty-five cents a pint, that's a lot of cheap whiskey, and you have to be sort of a brother to a guy to invest so much in his unrewarding pleasure.

Steve tried to get him to plead self-defense, but Bart got up there in front of his judge, looked at him hard and strong and said, "I killed a guy. I killed him because I wanted to. And I'd been thinking about it a long, long time."

About as long as he had known Doc. For ten years, he had been watching Doc torment the broken-down bums who crawled in and out of the cheap hotels and dirty rooming-houses in Ninth Street. These bums had made of Doc and his store the core of what was left of their small lives – a core of cheap whisky, barbiturates, marijuana, teasing portions of morphine. Doc had chiseled a fair lump of dough from the moral weaknesses of men, and he spread a little of it thin among them. All he asked in return was the crazy sort of pleasure he found in making them show their disintegration. Like Bennie Feezic did.

Bennie came into the store, stomped the snow off his worn shoes and shook the moisture out of his ragged cap. He gave Doc a sickly smile. Doc paid no attention to him, and just went on reading the sports page of the Times, opening and closing the pocketknife that had a spring blade. Bennie went back to the prescription counter. His yellow eyes carried hope to God that this was one day Doc wouldn't torture him. His cold, stiff hands had the sound of crumpling paper as he rubbed them together.

He didn't see Bart in his booth, and when Bart said, "Hello, Cokey," his eyes became fear-shot, like they always did when anyone gave him more than passing notice.

"Proud of yourself, aren't you," Bart sneered. "This is a fine winter evening to you."

"Aw, shut up," Bennie snapped.

"Think Doc's going to be real nice to you because you sent him that dame the minute she hit Ninth Street."

"Shut up, won't you?" Bennie whimpered.

Bart snorted. His mouth twisted in a contemptuous smile. "One of these days, Cokey, you're going to get too close to me. Then I'm going to pay you off for a girl named Mary Country."

Bennie pressed against the prescription counter. "Leave me alone, you lazy bum."

"Bum, he says," Bart laughed. "Sure, Bennie. But I didn't have to come down any. And I'm not scared Doc's going to get tired of playing with me."

"Doc's my friend," Bennie said.

"Your friend, my ragged pants!" Bart said.

Doc came back to the prescription counter. Bennie clawed at his coat sleeve, but Doc pushed him away.

"Clean the snow off the walk," Doc said to him. "People can't get in the joint."

Bennie backed up a step, and regarded Doc sadly.

"I'm sick, Doc," he whined. "If I get my feet wet –"

"I know, I know," said Doc. "Clean the walk or get out. No more stuff from me."

Bennie looked as if he would cry and started to follow Doc behind the counter. Doc turned and gave him a little shove.

"You heard what I said."

Bennie leaned across the counter. His eyes, wide with his fear, clung to Doc with a frenzied appeal, searching the thin, dark face for a sign of pity. He let out a pathetic whimper.

"But I did you a favor this morning. I sent you that cute little dish from the country. Figured she'd be good for your racket. I did you a favor, Doc. Ain't that worth somethin'?"

Doc's little eyes watched the torment form on Bennie's face.

"I had to send that little blossom away," he said.

Bennie fairly screamed. "No, Doc. Say you didn't. I was tryin' to do something' for you. I was tryin' to make you happy, Doc."

"I said I had to send her away."

He watched the tight leathery corners of Bennie's mouth begin to quiver, and traced the course of the little cokehead's spasms as they worked through his body. Soon, every thread that covered the miserable figure fluttered as the nervous system fell apart.

"Won't you let me have somethin' anyhow?" Bennie wailed.

Doc was deliberate with his next thrust.

"Wednesday. See me Wednesday night."

Bennie's hands were flat upon the counter. The yellow of his face deepened in his desperation.

"That's three days," he shrieked. "Three whole days an' nights. I'm too sick to wait, Doc." He put his head in his hands, half lying across the counter. His body shook with his sickening sobs. He stomped a foot. He doubled his fists and pounded the counter. While he wept, he howled, "I'm so sick, so sick. You're tryin' to kill me, Doc."

Doc watched him writhe. He was not moved to compassion or contempt. His cold, cruel eyes were simply fixed upon the dejected creature in front of him. Presently, he slapped Bennie sharply to break his hysteria and slipped a small white envelope between his fingers.

Bart waited until Bennie had run from the store and then said, without facing Doc, "I used to think there ought to be a way to rub out all the little Bennies in the world."

Doc came from behind the counter and stood beside Bart's table, fingering his knife, snapping the blade open and closing it.

"But while you were having your fun, I had another thought," said Bart. "It would be quicker to get rid of all the guys like you who keep dangling the Bennies on strings."

Doc lit a cigarette, and twisted one corner of his mouth to blow smoke out sideways.

"Someday," said Bart, looking up at him, "you're going to twist the wrong arm. What about the girl?"

"What, girl?"

"Quit stalling. I wasn't asleep when she came in this morning."

"Nice kid," Doc said.

"I heard you give her a fountain job," Bart said. "What do you really want her for?"

"The fountain," Doc said. He tilted his head back and blew smoke toward the ceiling. "She'll be good for the trade."

"You got her a room at the Ajax," said Bart. "You know it's no place for a kid like her. What have you got in mind?"

It wasn't a new plan Doc had in mind. The kid was naive. Doc would be kind to her, spinning the usual tale about the big money in posing for magazine illustrations. He'd start by getting her to pose a bit for the magazines, then a bit for art's sake. She'd drink a little for relaxation and maybe smoke some marijuana if it was needed. And before long, Bennie Feezic would be carrying bundles of her picture in some filthy pose to every dive in town.

"The kid needs work," Doc said. "I'm giving it to her."

"Bennie sent her to this street," said Bart. "She didn't know where she was going. The kid's clean, Doc, she trusts people. You knew she was green as hell."

"I didn't send for her," Doc said sharply.

"But you could have sent her away."

Doc flicked the ashes from his cigarette, lifted his chin up. "Just who the hell are you anyhow?"

Bart's anger was deep in his eyes, in the corners of his mouth. "I'm the only bum you've never been able to push around. I don't get down on my knees and snivel for you, and you don't like that. You wish I would so I couldn't hate your guts so much. You're afraid of me, Doc."

Doc sneered, "You're damned lippy for a bum."

"Yeah," said Bart, "For a bum I see things pretty straight, too. I have a funny way of falling in love with things I think ought to be on top. I mean to see that girl stays on top."

"Meaning what?"

"I'm not going to let you make a tramp out of her," said Bart. He pointed his thumb toward the floor. "Keep her out of your lousy basement. She isn't the kind."

Doc smirked. "It's a little late for you to be gin-happy over a dame."

Bart knotted his thick hands around his crutches. "I'm giving it to you straight. If I ever hear of that kid's face and body going out on one of your pictures—I'll kill you, Doc."

The skin over Doc's face tightened. He leaned over Bart's table, pressing his knuckles hard on its top.

"That's pretty big talk for a guy in your shape," he said. "And damned hard to back up."

After that Bart needed a drink. He touched Steve for another pint and slept if off in his usual booth. He was still asleep in his dark corner when the store opened to breakfast trade the next morning.

Harry was showing Mary Country around, trying to explain the work. It was easy to see she was lost in a fog.

She was shy, about eighteen, pretty in an open-country way. It was plain she had never spent much time away from home. Her hands belonged to chores of a house. When she dried a glass for Harry it sparkled an invitation to a man to be thirsty. She was sensitive and scared. Her fear was in her voice, her eyes, in her self-conscious movements. She belonged on Ninth street like a cat belongs in a bowl of gravy.

Bart stirred awake in his booth, snorting and rattling crutches and leg braces as he tried to move the kinks out of his body. He licked his whisky-fevered lips. He felt like biting off his tongue. The morning after threatening a guy's life is no time to hit him up for a drink. His consciences wouldn't let him touch Steve twice in succession, and Harry wouldn't give him any whisky. He would stake a bum to a feed, but a lot of soul-cleaning conversation had to be digested if he was asked for anything else.

Harry boiled an egg in the malted-milk can, toasted a slice of bread and poured a cup of coffee. Mary took it back to Bart's table and very carefully set the food down before him.

Bart stared up into her clean, innocent face.

"A kid couldn't get anything like this for Christmas," he said, and she smiled with a soft, decent mouth. "Usually, I'm lucky if it isn't thrown at me."

She treated Bart the same way even after she learned he never paid for his food or for anything else. On her third morning at the store, he got her to sit down at the table with him.

"I've been thinking a lot about you," he said. "You had some mighty nice Christmases at home." He caught the flicker of excitement in her eyes. "You did spend Christmas at home."

"Why do you think so?" she said.

"There's only one place a girl like you can come from. You don't fit in this town."

At first she was slow to admit she had been away from home only a few days, but Bart dug it out of her. He said every word he could think of to add to her homesickness, and when he started telling her how she had spent Christmas Eve the tears wouldn't stay in her eyes.

"Then you went to church. What did your preacher talk about? The little glass-eyed guy at the Mission said something about – let's see – people that walked in darkness have seen a great light—"

She took her handkerchief from her lips. "Isaiah," she said.

"And there was something about glass and fire –"

" 'And I saw what appeared to be a sea of glass mingled with fire'—Revelation."

"Revelation," Bart repeated slowly, watching her.

She wiped her eyes, blew her nose.

"Why did you leave, Kid?"

"I had to leave," she said.

"That I don't believe," Bart said.

Then she told him about her simple, sheltered life, the over-anxiety of her parents, how she had longed for cities and the opportunity to show the world how well she played the piano. When she finished talking, she looked down at the table.

"Now, you've made me act like a little girl."

"You look good that way," he said. "What else can you tell me?"

"I've told you everything."

"Except that you loved a boy," said Bart. "Your kind can't help it."

Her face colored slightly.

"Ok, skip the boy," Bart said. "But if you can play the piano, you've got a right to let people hear you. Only get off Ninth Street. It's the end, not the beginning, full of dead careers—all dead as grass in winter."

Mary didn't get off Ninth Street right away. She got along well with Doc's customers, had overcome some of her shyness. Though she still wore a homesick look bordering on sadness she put up a good front. To her there was no difference between the people she had known all her life and the people on Ninth street.

She moved from the Ajax to a rooming-house she let Bart choose for her. It did him a lot of good to be able to do something for her. She was generally good for him because he didn't suck the bottle so much when she was around. She was like a shaft of sunlight through a cellar window.

It made Bart sore because she liked Doc. He had a furious passion to find a way to tell her what Doc was really trying to do to her. She talked a lot about the boy she had left at home, and Bart clung to the stringy hope that the boy would come for her if she would let him.

"You were nuts about him," he said to her. "I don't know how he could be any other way about you."

She ran her finger along the crumb-filled crack in the table's surface. "He hardly noticed me."

"You told me he gave you that bracelet you're wearing," said Bart. "Boys don't spend their dough that way just to get rid of it."

She turned her eyes away from his." But if a boy cares for a girl—I mean, a bracelet alone doesn't tell everything. Something has to come from the boy himself."

"He was afraid of you," Bart said.

She faced him suddenly.

"He was afraid he'd dirty you with affection. There used to be boys like that. Have you written him since you came here?"

She shook her head. "I've wanted to—very much."

"If you asked him to come and get you—do you think he would?"

"I don't know. As a favor, yes. But because he loves me – Oh I don't know, Bart."

"You'll know if you try."

"I can't make up my mind," she said. "I want him, but I want my music, too. I'm not sure of him, Bart."

"If he's a right guy you'll get your music sooner than you will by yourself on Ninth street."

That night Bart found a new stake somewhere and was soused up in a different hole. No one saw him until noon the next day. Suddenly the door flew open, and Bart rattled in, wild-eyed and blue with cold. He looked as though he had betrayed a trust by not being at the store when Mary came to work.

"Where's the kid?" he barked savagely at Harry.

Harry nodded indifferently toward the back of the store. Bart looked relieved. He had been visualizing Doc's basement. He started back to his booth, then stopped. His big face became like a bull's.

He saw Bennie in the doorway of the room where Mary kept her coat. Then he saw Mary. She was dressed to leave, and Bennie was blocking her way, giving out a lot of cokey horseplay.

Bart put every ounce of strength he had into his crutches. As Bennie made a grab for Mary's hand Bart raised a crutch and gave him a fierce jab in the small of the back. Bennie grunted, stumbled forward, then whirled about like a mad cat.

Mary went around them and hurried out of the store.

When Bart started toward Bennie, he clutched a bottle of seltzer water from a case nearby. Bart's right crutch shot up, then crashed down on the bottle, shattering it.

Harry called from the front of the store, "What the hell's goin' on back there?"

Bennie cowered, then darted out and kicked one of Bart's crutches away. He plunged, hoping to knock Bart off balance. Bart caught his wrist, jerked it, and twisted it mercilessly. Bennie howled with pain, struck wildly at Bart's face with his free hand. Bart twisted the sprained wrist till Bennie sank to the floor.

Doc had come in and rushed back.

"What the hell?" he said to Bart. He glowered at Bennie on the floor. When he found out Bennie had been making passes at Mary he jerked the puling cokehead to his feet.

"I didn't mean nothin', Doc," Bennie whined. "Honest, Doc."

Doc clutched the lapels of Bennie's coat, backed him against the wall. He posed a trembling fist under Bennie's chin.

The skin of Bennie's face was wrung dry by his terror. "I was only tryin' to be nice."

"The kid's mine, understand?" Doc said. "Now, get out of here before I push your head through the wall. If you ever come back, I'll slip you a load of strychnine." He pulled Bennie to the doorway and shoved him through.

He turned his wrath on Bart, pushed his crutch toward him.

"I'm sick of you bums. Sick and tired of you. Get out. Find some place else to sleep off your drunks."

"Now, just a minute—" Bart protested.

"Get out," Doc shouted. "I don't want any trash around here that can't be swept up."

It was three days before Bart saw Mary, except at a distance. He stayed in the lobby of the Ajax most of the time, watching through the ceiling-high window, timing every movement she made in and out of the store. If she was a minute off schedule he sent Felix, the hotel porter, to buy his whisky and to report on her. He slept in the big horsehair chair by the window.

Friday evening Mary came to the hotel to buy some change for the store in time to hear Steve turn Bart down for a touch. Bart almost bumped into her when he turned to leave the desk.

"Hello, Kid," he said. "I was going out to get some medicine. Hamburgers don't set so well these days."

"Anything I can send you?" She asked. "There's a freezing mist and the streets are awfully slick."

"No thanks, Kid. I need the exercise."

"We miss you at the store. Why haven't you been in?"

"I had a job to do for the preacher," he lied. "Fixed his stove."

Steve laid her change on the desk. She pushed some coins for Bart his way.

Bart said, "Heard from the boyfriend yet?"

Her face became more alive. "He's coming tomorrow after work. I'm so thrilled, Bart."

"Going back?"

"I don't know," she answered.

"You'd better decide," he said. "There isn't much time."

She gave him a puzzled look.

"People don't stay as happy as you are now," he said. "There's a leak in the hourglass. Doc treating you ok.?"

She smiled, nodded. "He wants to take my picture. I didn't know—What's the matter? You seem angry, Bart."

Bart's lips tightened. His loose eyelids draped over his eyes like tent flaps.

"No," he said. He filled his big chest with air. His voice trembled a little. "No, just jealous, I wanted to do that. Let me know when Doc's ready. I'll help him."

When she had gone, he turned to Steve, crutches spread wide apart.

"It's time." He looked up at the age-stained Seth Thomas above the desk. Seven o'clock.

"Take it easy," Steve told him.

Felix went out and brought Bart a pint. It was gone by eight. Felix went for another. Bart put the bottle in his hip pocket. His eyes didn't move once from the front of Doc's store.

Bennie Feezix came by. He stopped, pressed his face to the coat of ice forming on the window. He came into the lobby, keeping a safe distance from Bart as he whined out his dejection.

"I'm sick, Bart. I know I'm dying."

Bart kept his eyes strained to peer through the darkness and icy mist at the lighted doorway of the store.

"I'll send you some flowers," he said sharply.

"Don't make fun of me," Bennie pleaded. "You don't know what it's like. All day and night I walk around on ice and snow—no place to lay down—nothin' to do but die like a dirty wet dog—cops at my tail every time I stop—Bart—" he whimpered.

He shivered with one chill after another. His lips were the color of indelible ink. One arm hung in a dirty sling.

"Get away," said Bart.

"For the love of Jesus help me get somethin', Bart. I need it bad. I've been all over town. Nobody'll give me anything. Make Doc give you some for me."

"Doc wouldn't give me peanuts," Bart said.

"You can make him. He's scared of you, Bart."

"Not because I want him to keep you souped up. Go make him yourself."

"He'll kill me, Bart. You heard him say he'd give me strychnine. I don't want to die. I want to get well and make somethin' of myself."

"Oh, hell, you little counterfeit," Bart said, facing him. "There isn't enough left of you to make a pile of chips. Get the hell out of here."

Bennie looked at him viciously. "All right, you four-legged sonofa—I'll get back at you. I'll get even."

He backed away, shaking a scrawny fist. He scrambled out of the lobby, slipped down the steps. He sprawled on the sidewalk. He got up, shook his fist again at Bart watching through the window, and in a sliding run disappeared down the alley.

Bart started to take a drink. Then he called Felix over and handed him the bottle.

"Take this," he said. "Now I'm sure it's time. When Bennie Feezic asks me a favor something's bound to happen."

He hung on his armpits at the window till nine. Then he said to Felix, "The kid's supposed to leave at nine. I haven't seen her. Go tell her I'm getting a cab to take her home."

"I'm supposed to quit at nine," Felix complained. "My feet's killin' me, an' I got three blocks to walk on that ice."

"If you go you can keep the whisky."

Felix went unwillingly and came back right away.

"She's workin' for Harry tonight," he said. "She'll be off at 'leven."

Bart sat down in the dilapidated chair. The foul hot air in the overheated lobby, the silence, the heat from the first bottle of whisky were working on Bart's brain. He had watched through the window so long that his eyes failed to focus. He rubbed his dry lips, yawned.

"If she isn't through that door by five after eleven, I'm going after her," he said.

He moved his big body slowly and clumsily to the edge of the chair. He held his crutches upright in front of him, like twin staffs, for support.

"What will you do?"

He saw Steve stare at his useless legs.

"What can you do?"

His lips twisted. He did not answer. He dozed.

"I'd better start moving around," he said. But his mind and his body had become separate units. There was no coordination.

"Tomorrow the boy's coming," he said, half to himself. "After tomorrow things will be alright."

Steve called and had a couple of hamburgers delivered. Bart ate his, then dozed again. Ten o'clock came. Steve finished his bookwork, then leaned back in his chair behind the desk. Seth Thomas mocked the dead silence of the lobby with hypnotic tocks. Bart's chin lay on his chest.

"Bart," Steve said, but there was no answer.

There was a big hunk of decency, a great love, in that wasted, shoddy body that depended on Steve to wake it. But Steve's had been a motionless life for the most part, his habits narcotic…

Bart woke him with a crutch. It was midnight. He looked at Steve fiercely, accusingly.

"Why in hell—" he said. He hobbled to the window, now covered by a sheet of ice like a great cataract He clattered back to the desk.

"Don't get excited," Steve said, flipping him a nickel. "Call where she lives. Maybe she's home."

Bart went to the phone booth and in a few seconds came out again. He was trembling with the fury in him.

He pounded a fist into the palm of his hand, hung motionless on his crutches for a minute while he tied his will and his nerves and his mind together. Then, swaying from side to side, like a man on stilts, he raced from the lobby, a grotesque mass of wild, clumsy movement driven by fury, and went out upon the icy street.

Bart," Steve shouted, but there was no way of telling if Bart heard.

The freezing mist, riding a fast wind, stung like sand. Bart crossed the slick pavement with his head down. If either crutch had slipped a fraction of an inch he'd have flopped in the middle of the street like a sack of potatoes.

Doc's store was dark except for a night light over the prescription counter. Bart grasped the cold brass of the door, shook it vigorously.

"By God, Doc," he said, pushing hard against the door.

He went to the back of the building, dark and rotten with slum fungus. Old stone steps, littered with junk and newspapers, all varnished with ice, led to the basement. The stair well was narrow, and Bart had trouble going down sidewise without entangling his legs and crutches in the refuse.

At the bottom he found the door secured by padlock and hasp. He backed up a few steps, then threw the weight of his body against the door. The rotten wood splintered at the hasp screws. Bart pushed the door open and faced Doc standing in the middle of the room.

Mary sat on a couch behind him, startled by the crash of the door. A bottle, a bucket of ice and a pair of glasses were on a cocktail table. Only a small lamp near the couch was lit.

When Bart pushed himself into the room Mary stood up and ran to him.

"Bart. What's the matter?" she cried. "What's happened?"

He pushed her toward the door. "Get out," he barked.

She was puzzled. She looked at Doc, then back at him.

"I don't understand, Bart."

"I said get out," he shouted. Go over to the hotel."

Doc had come forward.

"Like hell," he said furiously. He took hold of Mary's wrist, pulled her back into the room. He grasped Bart's wet coat at the throat and twisted it.

"I don't like punks trying to make a fool of me," he said.

Bart threw a thick fist into his face and pushed him away. Get your lousy hands off me."

Mary came toward them. "Bart. Doc. What—"

"Get the hell out of here, Kid," Bart cried angrily. "Can't you get anything through that thick skull?"

Doc had come back at Bart, slammed nasty sharp knuckles against his nose, knocking him back to the wall. Mary cried out with furious resentment.

"Don't you dare!" She began pounding on Doc's back with her two powerless fists. "Don't you dare hit Bart!"

Bart quickly moved his crutches out a few inches for better support locking the handles in his armpits.

Doc hit him again. Bart flung his arms out, but Doc stayed beyond reach. Doc came in and landed a third blow on Bart's mouth. It had lightning you could hear. When he came to deliver a fourth Bart lifted a crutch. A short, terrific push caught Doc under the ribs. He stumbled backward with a grunt, holding his side. He stood still a minute to regain his breath.

When he could speak his words were like cracks of a whip.

"Get out. I'll kill you if you don't get out."

Mary was terrified. She ran up the steps, crying as she went, "Do something. Stop them."

She vanished in the icy wind and dark.

Bart wiped the blood from his mouth with the back of his hand.

"I promised you that," he said deliberately. "This is for keeps, Doc.

Doc had removed his coat. He took slow steps toward Bart, his hands held threateningly in front of him. He was wise to the crutches. Bart's arms had to stay close to his body to help keep him erect. Doc was fully aware of his advantage. In swift darts of his slender body, he beat down Bart's defense and landed rapid blows on Bart's sweating, bleeding face. He reached low for a bale of power to slam at Bart's chin. But he was an inch too close. One of Barts hands flashed out and caught his belt.

He was against Bart now, raining ineffective blows against Bart's face. He tried to jerk away, to pull Bart off balance. Bart's armpits held his crutches like the jaws of vises. His free hand found Doc's throat, and there the fingers of steel strength that had drawn his heavy body for thirty years held fast.

Doc beat wild, savage blows against all parts of Bart's body and head. In terror and desperation, he took his knife from his pocket, snapped the spring blade open and struggled to hack at Bart's throat. Bart hugged close to him for protection. Again and again the knife bit shallow wounds into the flesh of his back, his arms, his ribs. The frenzied hacking brought on an unendurable breathlessness. Bart squeezed his eyes shut, sucked air through his teeth and winced with pain and madness.

Insanely Doc fought to release the hold on his throat. He tried to scream, but only weird, strangled grunts and gasps came from him. He kicked Bart's crutches away. Bart's entire weight hung on his belt and throat. Both men fell to the floor. Doc was on the bottom, and he kicked and squirmed like a slaughtered beast for the breath that would not come. He flung his knife from him, clawed fiendishly at Bart's face and neck, caught his hair, and pulled it with all his remaining strength. Slowly he sank into oblivion. His back arched as he tried feebly to throw the weight from him. Then his arms dropped and were still.

Bart waited before relaxing his girp, as if not realizing the struggle under him had stopped. He began to breathe again. Exhaustion overcame him. He rolled off Doc and lay flat on his back. He cried with pain, like a hurt boy. Blood drained into his throat and choked him. For a few seconds he dropped into unconsciousness.

He came to again with a gasp. "Mary. Thank God it's Saturday." He was brought back when he felt the warmth of Doc's hand. He licked his parched lips.

"God, I need a drink."

Steve heard him say so. He had reached the bottom of the steps in time to watch Doc die. Standing in the doorway, drenched by sweat despite the cold wind on his back, he wished he had guts enough to do something. But he had never learned to handle his crutches the way Bart did his.

The End

The Education of Eureka Dye

As he wiggled his short, round body through the small crowd that had loitered in front of the town hall throughout election day, a murmur rose, took shape, and blossomed into words that formed the voice of his people.

"How's the 'lection goin', Eureka? How's the tide runnin?"

Holding his flabby, bristly face high, cupping his lower lip to keep the tobacco juice from rolling down to his unshaven chin, Eureka Dye, the only representative of law in the hill-smothered village of Wobble Point, made his unchallengeable prediction.

"T' the Demeecrats, o' course! T' the Demeecrats!"

He swaggered up the steps of the ancient town hall, turned and gazed upon the heads of his followers. It was a magnificent feeling he had, and he enjoyed the delightful illusions of being an idol before a multitude. He pulled up his drooping, faded trousers, trying unsuccessfully to stretch them over his protruding belly. He maneuvered the wad of tobacco in his cheek to make room for free passage of the elaborate words of oratory with which he closed all election days. The thirty or forty Wobble Pointians who stood yawning, chewing, squinting and scratching looked up at him expectantly.

"Citizens and countrymen," he began, "you done yer dooty proud an' proper." Then he saw the small, withered figure of Maw Dye glaring fiercely at him from the front row.

"Git down from that high-falutin' jackass afore ye fall down, Eureka Dye," her tiny, sharp eyes were saying.

His spirit wilted and, quite somberly, feeling a good measure of disappointment in having to tie his ego down again, he called forth the two faithful townsmen who had served through the years as his watchers while he counted the votes.

Long, gaunt Burnside Peabody, official tally-keeper for twenty years, slumped into his chair at Eureka's left. Tess Brown, whose fat face wore a rosy beam of embarrassment, inched into her chair self-consciously and almost immediately felt the heavy drowse that possessed her on such occasions.

Eureka rubbed his grimy hands together and eagerly reached to unlock the battered ballot box.

"I git t'itchin' all over," he said, "when I watch them demeecrat votes stack up t' a gosh-a -mighty landslide."

"Reckon there'll be any change this year, Eureka?" said Burnside, pointing to the pile of ballots Eureka had poured upon the gavel-marred table. "Things have been happenin' sort o' fast lately."

"Ain't no change in Wobble Point votes," said Eureka. "I know them votes like I know good punkins, Burnside. They're solid Demeecrat, ceptin' fer Lily Terwilliger's an' Orph Cudbully's."

Counting the one hundred thirty-seven votes at Wobble Point was a mere formality. Except for two Republicans, Wobble Point was strictly a one-party town, which made the tedious procedure of ballot-counting markedly pointless. But Eureka's respect for the law was so deep-rooted he followed it to the last confusing semi-colon, insisting upon a vote-by-vote tally. Besides, he profoundly enjoyed examining the marks of his constituents. So familiar were they to him that the secrecy of the town's ballots was sheer fantasy.

"This here's old Ed Burke's, "he chuckled, lifting another from the pile. Then he laughed roundly as he thought of Ed's toothless mouth chopping out vituperation against evil politicians. "Allus makes a circle 'stead of a X. He's fer the ticket, but danged if he's fer the men on it."

It was a dull task for his watchers. Long ago, the wit in his remarks had dried up, and by the time Eureka had unfolded the fortieth ballot, Burnside and Tess were in a frame of mind to ignore the legal aspects of a complete count.

Burnside squirmed restlessly. "Looks t' me like there's a faster way than this t' count votes, Eureka. Ever'body knows there's only two Republicans. Can't we just count up the total now?"

Eureka sat upright. His chin shot forward. "Are you suggestin' we scrap the constitution o' the Yoonited States, Burnside?"

Burnside shrugged and shifted again in his chair. Eureka resumed his slow counting. Tess Brown's head nodded with the habitual dozer's short, limp dips into oblivion.

Suddenly, there was a long pause in Eureka's voice, long and, for him, odd. Burnside raised his head and looked at him. The abrupt descent of silence awakened Tess.

Eureka's eyes were fixed in a horrified stare upon the ballot before him. What he saw, he could not believe. He blinked his eyes and looked again. There was no deception. He had the feeling of being squeezed. The room seemed to be squatting down upon his round, plump shoulders.

"Good gosh a 'mighty!" he bellowed, jumping to his feet. "There's a element o' unrest in our mist!"

"There's a what?" Burnside shrieked.

"A revolution!" said Eureka, waving the ballot. "Danged dirty revolution!" said Eureka, waving the ballot. "Danged dirty revolution in the ranks!"

Burnside bent his long body across his corner of the table, reaching for the ballot. Tess Brown's face grew crimson, her eyes large. Her acquaintance with revolutions grew from a history-book version of the storming of the bastille, and Eureka's startling announcement struck her in the pit of the stomach and spiraled upward.

" 'tis the dirty doings o' rebellion," Eureka shouted, handing the ballot to Burnside. "Somebody's eased over t' the other side. That makes three fer "em now." He was in the grip of terror. How many more? Hastily he scrambled through the remaining ballots. With a sigh of relief, he mopped his sweating brow.

"There's a Demeecrat some'eres that's revoltin", he spat.

Burnside snorted at the red X in the wrong column on the ballot and exclaimed with mild profanity.

"Sure it's a Demeecrat, Eureka?" he said.

"Who else? We done counted Lily's an' Orph's."

"Could it be the new writer fella rentin' Sol Sudsy's cabin over in the woods?"

"He ain't legal," Eureka said irritably.

"Or maybe young Woody?" Burnside suggested naming the witless one of the village.

"He never votes, Burnside. Only time I seen 'im t'day he was botherin' t' know when the lynchin' was goin' t' start."

"Can't you reckonize the mark?"

Eureka pinched his lips and shook his head sadly. He snatched the ballot from Burnside, studied its mark again. "I seen it afore," he said. "I know I seen it afour, but danged if I can hook it onto anybody."

He sat down and propped his head up with his hands. He was tremendously aggrieved. It was the first time his trust in his people had been violated. His heart was heavy with the weight of deception.

"Somebody's sure gone plum batty," he mumbled. "It's a danged insult t' the party."

Suddenly he slapped his hand on the table, startling Tess Brown to greater wakefulness. "W got t' smoke out the varmint an' git t' the root o' this."

"No need t' be so jumpy," said Burnside. "One more out of a hunert an' thirty-seven won't wreck the party."

Eureka gathered himself into a foaming mass. He got up. He sat down.

"That ain't the way I got it figgered, Burnside," he growled. "Demeecrats is Demeecrats." He thumped the table with his fist. "The Demeecrats in Wobble Point ain't ever lost a vote. They've gone through times as bad as these here days o' adam-bombs an' Yoonited nations an' they ain't deserted the party. I ain't aimin t' let it happen now 'thout bruising my knucles a little. There's an unhappy Demeecrat loose, an' a unhappy Demeecrat is the orneriest sort o' critter alive."

"What ought we' t' do? Said Burnside.

"Can't do nothin' legal," Eureka said. "We got t' find the varmint some way an' git at the cause o' his unhappiness. Then we edicate him back."

"How you figger t' do that, Eureka?" said Burnside.

Eureka stared thoughtfully at the dusty, worn floor, pulling at the sagging flesh of his lower chin. Presently, his eyebrows lifted.

"A investigatin' committee, that's what," he said. "A secret investigatin' committee, Burnside."

The worry on Tess Brown's face had deepened. Her mind was burdened with the scrambled horror of Eureka's words about frightful revolutions, unrest, rebellion, lynching, varmints wrecking the party. She squirmed uneasily.

"I better go now," she said with a slight quiver in her voice. "The kids is all alone an' I got t' see they get t' bed. Besides, the countin's about done, an' it looks honest 'nough t' suit me."

Eureka let her go. His eagerness to begin plans for his secret investigating committee forced the remaining ballots out of his mind.

At midnight, Burnside announced he was going home. Eureka continued to ponder, hardly aware Burnside was shuffling out of the room.

It had been a proud day for him, and he could not bear the thought of its coming to a dismal end. Election day was his day of glory, the only day he could rise to his full official stature before the eyes of his people. The dismay he felt because of the swing of another vote to the opposition's side was as great as if he faced complete ruin.

He thought of Maw Dye. He dared not confront her with the weight of a lost vote bearing down upon his shoulders.

Serves ye right, ye conceited little horn-tooter," she would say, shaking her bony finger in his face. "I been a'tellin' ye, Eureka Dye, ye been pickin' yer punkins ahead of ripenin'. Ye been thinkin' too long that nobody in Wobble Point'd vote anyway but yer way."

It was no secret that Maw Dye was the power behind Eureka's political throne. She had the swift, sparklike movement of an eighty-year-old delicate frame, commanding the respect of all the town's citizens. The symbol of her power, a sizeable chunk of railroad tie, stood behind the stove in her kitchen. More than once during Eureka's twenty years in office, she had spit on her hands, grasped the chunk of wood, and wielded it mightily to keep Wobble Point's party leadership well in line.

One day, she put away the big stick, forsaking it for the more modern methods of treating the waywardness of her youngest son.

"Too stern," she decided. "Eureka's sensitive, too intelleegent to let his bad spots be beaten out of him."

The bad spots she saw in Eureka were his cocky swagger, his walk of a pompous goose, and his absolute dead certainty of winning any election, hands down. She had devoted half her life to raising a son of whom no ill could be spoken, and she had enjoyed a large measure of success.

"But he's too derned conceited," she declared. "I'd rather he'd be a chicken-thief than have him go 'round with that 'I done it' look ever' time the Democrats win."

Curing him was not a job for the big stick. It required the wile of woman, the hidden power of suggestion and unconscious persuasion, the art of subtlety.

When Burnside found Eureka the following day, he was curled up in the corner of the town hall, wrapped in deep, chilly slumber. He roused him by prodding the fat around his ribs several times with the toe of his boot.

Eureka sat up, grunted, and slowly blinked his eyes open.

"Been here all night?" Burnside asked.

Eureka massaged his stiff knees. "Didn't want t' wake up Maw," he said, yawning. "She'd a swore I was over in Sedgwick 'sky-hooten' with the sheriff. Now you can prove I spent all night in the town hall workin' on important party business."

"Still skeered o' yer maw, Eureka?"

"No, I ain't. She's getting' along in years an' I like t' humor her."

"Sure it ain't that railroad tie yer humorin'," Burnside said.

Eureka looked at him disdainfully and ignored the taunt. He wheezed and stooped over to lace his boots.

"I done a little more figgerin' after you took out last night," he said. "Seemed I could think better. Know who our varmint is?"

"Who?"

"Come t' me just like that!" He snapped his fingers. "I says, 'Eureka, the foot fits the shoe,' I says."

"Who is it, Eureka?"

Eureka straightened up. "Lem Bradley's boy, Luke."

"What makes you think so?"

"Well, ain't he just come home from college this year? An' ain't some o' them college squirts full o' ridickerlous ideas? He's been free with his talk lately, an' he's got leanin's toward bein' the fantastic sort."

He wormed his fat hand into a tight trousers pocket and produced a crumpled postcard. "Here's some eveedunce," he said. "When

Luke dawned on me as the guilty varmint, I went rummagin' around Bradley's trash can in some perlimeenary investigatin'."

Burnside took the card and laboriously read its message. "Why, it's t'night, ain't it. Eight o'clock meetin', Luke's house—Lookee there at them funny letters, Eureka. What you reckon they say?"

"Never seen 'em afore. Some silly sign his Republican club at the college uses, no doubt. An' see under his name? He's secketary o' the danged outfit."

"What you aim t' do?" Burnside asked. "His old man owns ever' mortgage in town, an' you know he'd raise nine kinds o' hell of anything happened t' his boy."

Eureka thumped the table with his knuckles. "Lem ought t' be glad in the long run. If he knowed Luke was a rebel he'd burn his britches off."

"You goin' t' tell him?"

"Not yet," said Eureka. "T'night we'll do some more secret investigatin'."

Burnside shook his head. "Don't seem t' be very secret no more. The whole town's stirrin' up a little about the varmint that's runnin' loose. Reckon Tess must a been on the phone all night."

"Might a knowed that," Eureka snorted. "Gals go breezin' around about things they only half hear. This business ain't fer nobody 'cept us politicians workin' t' keep the party t'gether."

"Nobody's right sure what the varmint is. Olga Mape's girl told Letty Todd's there's a giant loose here that's got the whole Yoonitee States skeered o' its shadder."

"Olga Mape's girl is looney," Eureka said.

"An' there's some thinks a spy's set himself up in the old dyneemite shack over by the dam."

Eureka groaned. "Gosh a' mighty. You go tell Tess Brown t' keep her blamed mouth shut."

Burnside grinned. "There's a few o' the boys waiting' at yer house t' be depetized."

"Depetized!" Eureka howled. "What fer?"

Burnside took a plug of tobacco from his pocket, bit off a chunk and passed the plug to Eureka. "Can't be a revolution 'thout a good scrap."

Burnside squeezed his face between his hands and moaned. "Some o' the boys asked if you sent for the Yoonitee States marshal."

Eureka swung around. "Is ever'body tetched? What they think is goin on? Rebellion?"

Burnside nodded. "That's what they say."

Eureka grasped him by the arm. His entire being seethed. "You got t' stop this foolishness, Burnside. Tell ever'body this business about varmints an' revolutionists is only Tess talkin' in her sleep.

"What you aim t' do, Eureka?"

"I'm goin' over t' Sedgewick, that's what. If I face the boys now an' don't tell 'em what's goin' on they'll swear I'm holdin' out on 'em. Then they'll git t' grumblin' an' stir up some trouble just for the hell of it. You git 'em smoothed off an' I'll meet you t'night at eight o'clock behind Bradley's barn."

He squashed his hat on his head and rubbed his face vigorously to limber it up. "Revolutions! Rebellion! Plain cracked, that's what." As he started out the rear door of the hall, he was stopped abruptly by a poignant thought. "Tell Maw I'm on secret dooty fer my party so she won't be worryin' that railroad tie t' death.

Promptly at eight o'clock he stole stealthily through the shadows of the great naked elm trees at the side of Bradley's house. A cold, glooming moon shone over his shoulder, and he clung to objects of girth so anyone peering from a Bradley window would not see him sneaking furtively along his way. Instead of the law he felt like a man pursued, or like a prowling conspirator working his feet cautiously toward a secret rendezvous.

"Conspirator, yep," he thought.

The word struck his fancy. Almost immediately, he was transformed into another person. No longer Eureka Dye, he was a black-hooded figure from the pages of medieval history, and the barn he sought was a dark, dripping subterranean passage wherein his fellow plotter lurked. Reaching the barn where Burnside was waiting, the charm of his nocturnal daring ended abruptly when he stumbled and sprawled in the manure pile.

He heard Burnside's unrepressed shout of laughter. He scrambled to his feet excitedly and shushed Burnside to be quiet.

"Hankerin' fer a load o' buckshot?" he said, panting up to Burnside. He brushed away the clinging crumbs he had carried from the pile.

They had a clear view of the Bradley front door. Four cars were parked in front of the house. A light glowed in a window of an upstairs rear room.

"That must be the meetin' place," Eureka whispered. "I'd give a perty t' be up on that porch roof."

They stole quietly away from the protection of the barn toward the Bradley back porch. Eureka stood in the shadows of an old walnut tree and surveyed the rear wall of the clapboard house, watching the lighted window.

"Remember, this ain't right legal," he said to Burnside in a strained whisper. "Don't let yer party loyalty run away with yer wits."

Burnside found a down drain from the Bradley guttering and called Eureka over to him. "this here goes right up by the winder. Get up high 'nough an' you can hook yer foot t' the porch roof fer support. Then you can hear ever'thing that's said."

Eureka took hold of it, gave it a couple of experimental jerks and put a foot against the house.

"Not you," Burnside protested. "You'd jerk out the whole derned end o' the house."

Eureka unwillingly relinquished the special investigating privilege of his office to this light man. Burnside took off his boots, spit on his hands and started the ascent to the porch roof. He finally fixed himself in place with no more noise than the squeak of a rusty nail.

Silence. Waiting. Eureka's neck grew stiff from holding his head back. He was impatient for a report on the proceedings of the meeting. Nothing came out of the room but muffled laughter. No mention was made about Republicans or Democrats. Only some talk about girls. Burnside's legs stiffened, yearning for a change in position. He tried to maneuver them noiselessly. For a second, they lost their hold; his total weight was thrown on the downspout. There was a retching wail as rusty nails were torn from their sockets in the aged wood of the house.

Sh-h-h-h" Eureka warned.

"Tain't me," said Burnside. "Whatever it is don't sound good." He seemed uneasy. Again, he tried to maneuver; once more, the suffering nails bore the burden of his weight.

Then the downspout collapsed, pitching Burnside on top of Eureka. Both sprawled. Sections of pipe and gutter showered down danced clumsily and stiffly from one end to the other, bouncing against the porch, scraping the cement sidewalk. Eureka thought the noise was endless, more horrible than any he had ever heard. Barking dogs and shrieking women could not have created a greater uproar.

The window at which Burnside was listening opened and the head of a young man popped out.

"Prowlers, Luke," it said, spying the two figures tangled on the ground and splashing in the moonlight. "Down by the porch. Get your gun."

Eureka and Burnside struggled fiercely to become free of each other, finally got to their feet and dashed off in different directions. In a few seconds, Luke and fifteen other young men were chasing after them.

Burnside got caught in a hog wallow enclosed by a four-foot fence. Eureka was off like a brisk wind, unmindful of fences. He fairly swished as he dashed against the chill breeze. His hat blew off, and his head gleamed like a ripe pumpkin. His round melon body had difficulty keeping up with his short, fat legs. He fled across the three-acre rutabaga field into the rough, new-plowed ground, gasping. His mouth drooped open, fine streams of tobacco juice trickled from his lips and flew off his whiskery cheek in tiny droplets. He entered the stubbly cornfield like a hounded hare, his shouting pursuers close behind him. One of his boots came off, throwing his mad gallop into a lopsided gait. His bare toes were snagged by the fiendish, sharp stubble of the stripped field. He fell headlong to the ground, rooting his face in the hard earth.

Luke and the entire party of the opposition piled on top of him. When they unscrambled themselves, Eureka tried to speak to Luke, but his tongue stuck to his teeth. The boys surrounded him and prodded him back to the house, greatly amused when they learned the identity of their captive. Even Luke, pressing Eureka for an explanation, broke out in chuckles. Eureka was encouraged by the attitude of his captors. This had the makings of something that could be laughed off.

Then, as he neared the house, his heart hung in him like a sashweight. Marching toward the Bradley front yard was a group of Wobble Point men armed with shotguns and torches. Lem was in the middle of the yard, waving his arms up and down and pacing back and forth in front of Burnside. His rage thundered in Eureka's ears. When Eureka was brought nearer, Lem turned upon him.

"Eureka Dye!" he bellowed, knotting his hands and pushing them close to the bruised nose of the trembling official. "You hog-bristled little ball of putty! This is an out-RAY-geous demonstration, a dis-GRACE-ful exhibition!" the words dripped from him like the slow dropping of hot lead. "What kind of rubbish are you patronizing your constituents with now? What is the meaning of this FIEND-ish mob!"

Eureka glanced at the mob, now milling up before the house. He turned a withering look upon his barefoot special agent, silently threatening to skin him for dropping the Bradley name in the middle of the wild talk about varmints and revolutions. He stammered a confused explanation of his mission.

Lem shrieked, stomped his feet, sucked in a new breath. "What a public servant you are, Eureka Dye, you're a ruined man! Politically, you are a roo-ined man!"

Eureka held out a shaking hand. "Calm yerself, Lem," he stuttered. "Calm yerself down. No use gettin' het up over somethin' too prematoor t' make head or tail of."

"Calm myself down! When you and this pea-brained spy of yours come sneaking about my peaceful house—Calm myself down!"

Eureka fumbled for the postcard he had found in the Bradley trash can.

"I didn't want t' do it this way, Lem." He said with bravado. "But yer forcin' my hand." He passed the card to Bradley. "Here's the soopreme piece o' eveedunce t' bear out the facts o' all this commotion."

Bradley looked at the card. Luke and a couple of the boys peered at it over his shoulder. Their laughter rang merrily through Eureka's dilemma.

"Why, you officious, potbellied, tankheaded goose," Lem howled. "My son's fraternity meeting and you – you—" He pushed his sweating, purple face into the dusty one of Wobble Point law. "I'll have the real law-- the genuine United States law – on you for this. Maybe the marshal will like knowing how you and your prowling fathead confederate tamper with the ballot boxes. How will you explain that, you low-bred hound of a swizzle-britches!"

At that moment, Maw Dye came forward from the rear of the crowd, holding her black scarf tight about her head with a hand of knobby knuckles.

"Howdy, son," she said gravely. Poor boy, she thought. She got him fixed up good this time. He was trying so hard to do what he thought was right, and in the doing he had tripped over her own foot. He needed her now more than ever. She called upon every resource of strength.

Eureka's spirits rose. She brought strength to his sagging muscles. Her pinched little face was firm with courage in the flickering light of the torches.

"That's m'boy ye said them ugly words to, Lem," she said. "While I'm mighty agin what he's done t'night I ain't aimin' fer him t' be whipped by nobody but me."

Len stooped over and shook his finger in her face. He began shouting at her, but she raised her voice to a high-pitched squeak.

"Eureka's headstrong," she said, "He feels his dooty an' his loyalties powerful hard. I tried t' stop this here mob, but once Eureka's set for somethin' there ain't no stoppin' people from follyin' him into a mess. He's the leader type."

"Leader type or not," Lem yelled. "Things like this can't happen to me. Do you think I'm going to laugh off sneaking prowlers and front-yard mobsters with lethal weapons? Not even for you, Maw Dye!"

"Ain't askin' for favors, Lem," she said. "Just want ye t' weigh the facts. Callin' the marshal might make somebody look a little foolish when he gets the straight o' this. I'm eighty years old, Lem, an' I've knowed you sixty of 'em. You're my kind o' people, an' I think you'll see this my way."

"I can't see anything but having this sort of thing stopped. I know my rights, and I demand they be recognized."

"So does Eureka," she said. "An' I aim t' see they are. You an' ever'body in Wobble Point knows he don't have t' change no votes. This town's been Demeecrat since it was settled, long afore Eureka's time, an' there ain't ever been mor'n two votes agin 'em. That's what got Eureka all fouled up. The town's so derned Demeecrat he growed too sure o' himself. Allus been so certain of a Demeecrat landslide t' impress them city poleeticians with he ain't been fitten t' live with."

She turned and scowled at her son. "Pride goeth afore the fall," she said; and somehow in the squeak of her voice she managed to inject thunder.

Facing Lem again she went on. "I'm here t' say how sorry I am ye got mixed up like this. If yer willin' Eureka'll apoleegize. If things had been thought through proper this wouldn't a happened. I ain't sayin' who betrayed m' boy wit the stray vote. Nobody's business. I know 'twasn't Luke. Maybe it was somebody tryin' t' point t' Eureka the errin' of his ways. Maybe it was a lesson taught with suttlety –an' the suttlety misfired. Leastways, that's the way I got it figgered, an' t' my mind it's perty good figgerin'."

Luke and the boys were caught up in the humor of Eureka's plight. They gave Maw a rousing cheer.

"I ain't got a right t' lay hand t' the others," she said, waving toward the torchbearers "But I can still chastise my own when he's needin' it. Eureka done mighty wrong t'night, even for the sake o' party loyalty, an' I aim t' fix him so he won't make the same mistake agin."

Lem looked at the tiny, gnarled hand she held out to him and refused to take it.

"'Tain't a big hand, Lem," she said. "But it's allus been a helpin' one an' never done a hurt. It's a good hand t' be friendly with."

Lem swung about and looked at the mob. His jaw clamped tight. He glanced at Burnside, pale and humble with guilt. Then he faced Eureka, cowering beside Maw. They added up to too much for him to bear. He clenched a fist, raised it, and opened his mouth to bellow again.

Luke took his arm and gently pushed it back to his side. "No use catching cold, Pop. This is the best meeting the boys have ever had."

The boys had come out for the chase in their shirtsleeves. Now they were feeling the cold and started returning to the house.

Lem's body relaxed. His fist unfolded. Maw's eyes clung to him. He took her little fingers and squeezed them.

"I knowed ye'd be fair," she said.

Turning to the gawking crowd, she ordered them away. "Git on home with them fires an' guns afore ye do harm with 'em."

Taking hold of one of Eureka's ears, she jerked him out of his official status and pushed him ahead of her.

"You git, too, ye meddlin' young scamp!"

She felt in the pocket of her long skirt for the stub of red pencil. She shook her head conclusively.

"Reckon I'm old-fashioned," she thought. "I should a stuck t' the big stick.

The End

My Pop and Uncle Emil

By Raymond Johnson

My pop always made fun of me when I got a little hurt or something, and I'd bawl awhile to get it out of my system. He said men didn't bawl, and I'd have to learn how to take a hurt in my stride.

"Boy," he said, "if you keep yourself wet with tears, you'll never amount to anything. You will always be a boy no matter how old you get."

He always called me Boy. My name is Hampton, but he never liked that name, and I didn't either, but I put up with it because Mom liked it. There was something strong about the way Pop said Boy, and it made me feel like I was his pal. He only called me Hampton when he was mad and looked like he was going to wham the daylights out of me.

That's the way he looked the Sunday before Uncle Emil came. Mrs. Carmichael was talking to him over the back fence. She's our next-door neighbor. She had a mad wrinkle between her eyes. I acted like I was busy at the end of the yard by Mom's peony bed, but I was only fingering around, straining my ears to hear what she was saying. I had a good idea of what she was telling Pop, but I wanted to hear how she said it. Pretty soon, she went into her house, and Pop turned from the fence, looking violent.

"Hampton," he said.

If you've ever heard wood-splitting thunder during a summer storm, you know how that name sounded to me.

"Come here, Hampton," he said.

I felt shaky all over, like maybe a bunch of grasshoppers were chasing each other inside me, and while I was easing toward him, I tried to figure out whether he was whipping mad or just scolding fiercely. He shook a finger under my nose and said something about respect for other people, and just as I thought he was only scolding fierce, he whacked me a good one on the seat of the pants.

I truly gained respect for Pop's hand that day, and I guess it was then I decided not to mock Mrs. Carmichael anymore when she said petunia. The way she said it was pee-too-nya, and it always made me think of pee-you-too-nya, and that's the way I said it so the fourteen women in her garden club could hear me.

Mrs. Carmichael had the idea she was aristocratic or something. She never had any kids, and all she ever did was pull weeds out of her flower beds. She always looked like something was pinching her. Mr. Carmichael worked for a railroad and had a pass, and they always took trips, but Mrs. Carmichael tried to make the other women on our street think they paid their own way.

She thought her pee-too-nya was the best in the world, and every month in the summer, her garden club met in the shade of our maple trees. You know how the shade of your trees always flops over somebody else's yard. Well, those women sat in our shade and fanned themselves and listened to Mrs. Carmichael talk about some new pee-too-nya she had that cost more than anybody else's. She was so darned uppity about those pee-too-nyas that it made you want to pull them up by the roots. And if I didn't have so much respect for other people, I sure would have, too, when she told Pop we'd have to get rid of Alec. That was the summer before Uncle Emil came.

Alec was one of my ducks. I had six of them. I was sick all winter, and when Spring came and I was able to be out in the sunshine, Pop bought me these ducks that were the cutest things you ever saw. Pop built a real house for them with windows and everything a house has except furniture and a bathroom, and he built a concrete pond where I sailed the boats I made out of shingles when the ducks weren't swimming. It was a small pond. Pop could do anything, and everything he did was so nice, and I guess that's one reason I liked to have him call me Boy.

I sure loved those ducks. They must have known how much fun I got out of them because they sure strained themselves to make me laugh. The way they stretched their necks and flapped their wings while they chased butterflies round and round the yard, all six of them hopping over each other and wrestling for the same butterfly, was enough to make anybody laugh except Mrs. Carmichael.

She called them horrid, smelly things, and Alec didn't like it a bit. If any of them was my favorite Alec was. He would watch Mrs. Carmichael wiggle her mouth about her pee-too-nyas, then he'd turn away disgusted and quack something that sounded like, "Aw, shut up." Since ducks aren't supposed to show respect for other people, I just let him keep on doing it.

What Mrs. Carmichael hated most about Alec was the way he nibbled at her pee-too-nyas. He stuck his nose through the fence, nipped off a petal and gobbled it down like he would a fat cricket. Even while Mrs. Carmichael was looking, he dared to do that, and it made her so mad she would have hopped up and down if she hadn't thought she was so aristocratic.

One day, she wasn't outside to throw something at Alec when he stuck his nose through the fence, and those pee-too-nyes tasted so good that he ate and ate until sixteen of those double extra frilly ones disappeared down him. Pop tried to tell Mrs. Carmichael that maybe the bugs did it, but she only got madder and said there wasn't a bug in her place.

It's that horrid smelly animal, she said, and she walked away from the fence mumbling something about people who have dirty things messing up their yards.

That's why I wondered how Pop dared to bring Uncle Emil home.

Well, I sure loved those ducks, and when they were gone, I just bawled like a baby, and I didn't care if I never grew up to be a man. I couldn't blame it all on Mrs. Carmichael either because Pop enjoyed his duck dinners too much.

If I didn't like my Pop so much, I sure would have hated him hard while he was smacking his lips over those ducks. I didn't eat for a month, I'll bet, and every time I sat down to the table, the bawling foamed up inside me and spilled all over my face.

When the day came to eat Alec – I knew it was Alec by the way his neck was twisted like it did when he looked at me to see if I was laughing at him—why, I just wrinkled up and hardly had strength enough to go up to my room. Pop came up and patted me on the back of the head and started talking about how to be a man, and all I could do was bawl. Go away, go away, go away, like a woman did in a movie I saw once when she got mad at her boyfriend. No, sir, right then I didn't care if I never got to be a man.

When Pop brought Uncle Emil home, I didn't care for him much. He was cute in a way, but he was clumsy, and he didn't look funny chasing butterflies because he never chased any. All he did was dig holes with his nose in Mom's peony bed after a hard rain, and Mom would get mad at Pop, and Pop would say it didn't do any harm. Besides, Uncle Emil was a good pet for me, but if I knew my Pop I'll bet he looked at Uncle Emil like he thought he would make a good Christmas dinner.

The first time Mrs. Carmichael saw Uncle Emil in our backyard she looked like she had swallowed a firecracker that exploded as soon as it hit bottom. She got purple in the face, and her eyes looked like big hailstones with blue spots on them. She told me to have Pop come out in the backyard, and when he did, she forgot that she thought she was aristocratic, and she yelled at Pop at the top of her voice and called him everything but the name that makes men want to fight. Pop didn't say anything, but he was pretty mad when he went into the house.

"Now I'll keep Uncle Emil just for darned meanness," he said to Mom, only he didn't say darned.

The next day a man came out from the City Hall and told Pop he would have to get rid of Uncle Emil because it was against the law to keep him inside the city limits. If anybody besides Mrs. Carmichael had snitched, Pop probably would have got rid of Uncle Emil and forgotten him, but he felt that he had been double dog dared and said he wouldn't give up Uncle Emil until hell froze over, which I guess meant never.

He looked up the law, he read it about a hundred times and then he called old Judge McDaniel, who belonged to Pop's lodge, to make sure he was right. He was so happy he almost did a flip-flop when he got through talking to the judge, and then he went out to the backyard, holding the law book open to the right place.

Mrs. Carmichael was talking to her garden club when Pop stormed out the back door. She got sort of white-faced when Pop walked up to the fence with his law book, and she pretended not to see him.

Pop was nice and polite in a mad way.

"Mrs. Carmichael," he said, "May I have your respectful attention one moment, please?"

Then he rattled off the law word for word.

"In short, Mrs. Carmichael," he said when he finished, "The law says one cannot keep pigs—P-i-g-s—to breed, feed or to sell, but nowhere can it be interpreted to mean that one cannot keep a pig—P-I-G-- Mrs. Carmichael—as a pet."

Well, Mrs. Carmichael looked like she was going to get sick, and I felt real sorry for her. Even if she was arrogant, most of the time, her feelings had been hurt in front of her garden club. I guess Pop felt wicked the next day because he asked Mom if a delivery truck from the candy store had been out our way.

Mom said, "It's a funny thing, but Mrs. Carmichael and I both received a box of candy from some mysterious person."

Pop said, "Well, that is odd," and then he sat down to read the newspaper, looking sort of satisfied with himself.

Uncle Emil must have known what Pop went through for him because he fell head over heels in love with Pop. Pop couldn't do anything in the yard without having Uncle Emil snuggling up to him and making a sort of snortle sound with his nose. Every step Pop took Uncle Emil was at his heels, and when Pop went in the house, Uncle Emil looked peeved because he couldn't go in, too.

You could see Pop was a little that way about Uncle Emil. He fixed a nice place for him to sleep under the back porch, hosed him off once a week and took a personal interest in what he ate. Once he told Mom that maybe he'd groom him for a blue ribbon, but Mom acted like she thought he was being silly, and he didn't say any more about it.

Mrs. Carmichael never complained anymore after she had the law read to her, but once I was sitting under the grape vines where she couldn't see me, and she came up to the fence, leaned her head over and sniffed around like she was trying to see how bad our yard smelled. I don't think she smelled anything, though, because Pop is pretty particular about such things.

One day, Pop said he would take Uncle Emil over to Mr. Downing's barn. I heard Mr. Downing tell Pop that Uncle Emil ought to be decapitated or something, and the day Pop took him, I got worried because I thought they were going to cut off Uncle Emil's head. Pop told me to stay home, but I followed him over to Mr. Downing's anyway. I wasn't in love with Uncle Emil, but I wasn't going to let them cut off the poor pig's head if I could help it. When Pop found out I had followed him, he let me stay, but he made me promise to keep out of the barn. He laughed when I told him he'd better not cut off Uncle Emil's head; then he said they weren't going to hurt him much. But good gosh, you should have heard all the pig howling that came out of that barn. You'd have thought Uncle Emil was being turned the wrong side out alive.

Pretty soon, Pop came out of the barn, and he stood there looking at me like I was a ghost or something. I thought he was going to cry. In a minute Mr. Downing came out of the barn, and he was laughing like he thought Pop was funny.

"Can't take it, huh?" Mr. Downing said, and that's exactly what Pop said to me the time I hit my thumb with a hammer while I was making a martin house.

Pop picked up Uncle Emil in his arms and carried him home, and he put him in his place under the back porch. Every twenty minutes he came out of the house to see how Uncle Emil was. He didn't pay any attention to me for two days. The first thing he did when he came home from work was to ask Mom how Uncle Emil was, and before she could answer, he'd see for himself.

Uncle Emil got well all right, and then Christmas started coming slow, like a heavy load up a long hill, and I got too busy hoping and wishing to think about him until one afternoon, I came home from school to find Pop talking to Mom about him.

"But I've already invited everybody related to us for Christmas dinner," Mom said.

"We could get a different pig, one we don't know so well," Pop said.

Mom looked like she was peeved. She said, "You're being ridiculous about that animal. Sam the butcher was telling me the other day Mrs. Carmichael is circulating a petition in the neighborhood. She says she won't live another summer next to pigs – P-I-G-s," she said.

"Oh, hang Mrs. Carmichael," Pop said.

Mom said, "Remember, not everyone falls in love with pigs."

Pop said, "We could get another pig for dinner and send Uncle Emil out to some farm where he can be happy without Mrs. Carmichael butting in."

I felt sorry for Pop. Mom always wore him down to thin batter when he argued with her.

Mom said, "Whoever heard of boarding out a pig? You may as well know the truth," she said, "I'm a little tired of all this affection for Uncle Emil."

Pop snorted and left the house, and he pouted for a week. When the time came to send Uncle Emil to the butcher's, Pop disappeared, and he stayed away all day, and after that I never saw him go near the door to Uncle Emil's house under the porch. He never laughed any more, and he didn't seem to care what I wanted for Christmas. When I asked him if we could have a big tree, he said, "Hampton, you can have a dozen trees."

Now, when Pop doesn't complain about spending money on Christmas trees, he's just plain gone.

On Christmas morning, his smile seemed a bit brighter as I unwrapped my presents, and he affectionately called me "Boy" several times, filling me with warmth. Laughter filled the air, and then the man came from the place where they roast pigs on a spit and Pop got mighty sober.

All of Mom's relatives and all of Pop's relatives started coming for dinner and Pop got gloomier and gloomier. The noisier they were, the sadder he was, and I think he hated them all because they had come to eat Uncle Emil.

Uncle Emil was sure beautiful, with baked apples and prunes and apricots all around him and on top of him, and everybody smacked their lips and said they'd been waiting a long time for this and wouldn't wait a minute longer.

My plate came to me stacked up almost to the ceiling and I was awful hungry because I felt so good. Everybody talked and laughed and said how good everything was. Then I looked at Pop. He was only staring at poor, torn-up Uncle Emil. I guess all he could think of was the way Uncle Emil used to snuggle his snout against him when he wanted attention. He watched everybody fill their mouths, and suddenly, I knew how he felt. All his relatives and all Mom's relatives and Mrs. Carmichael and her petition had ganged up on him. I wasn't hungry anymore, and every time I looked at Pop, my nose stung, and my eyes got watery.

It's funny how you can get crazy in love with something like a pig. I know how I was about Alec, and when I saw Pop was like that about Uncle Emil, I began to get foamy inside. I guess Pop never really did get over being a boy.

The End

A Son for Amanda

By Raymond Johnson

Except for Paul, her son, who sat now without heritage, Amanda Pearson had no family. But the old church she had attended for fifty of her eight-seven years was not large enough to hold the crowd of people who came to look upon her for the last time. Many sat through the service with a feeling that was not of sorrow but more of self-rebuke, for they had said things about Amanda that never could be retracted, and they felt now that they need not have been said.

"Plain crazy. She ought to be put away. For her own good, you know."

At her funeral were perhaps twenty who recalled with discomfort of conscience that they had forgotten or put off too long the repayment of their debts to Amanda. She had financed their journey to this country from Sweden, and provided them with shelter, food, medical care, and assistance in establishing their new lives. A score of others remembered smaller debts, like the Potters, whose baby was buried at Amanda's expense, the Stranges, whose table never wanted while Strang was laid up with a broken back, the Petersons, the Olsons, and Oscar Carlson—No, Oscar Carlson's thoughts were not theirs. He had repaid it many times over.

He sat looking at the flowers banked behind Amanda's casket, his large body erect, his white-topped head high. His eyes were misty, and there was a thickness in his throat. He half turned as if to speak to the young man sitting beside him, but he checked himself.

His thought had been replaced by another, then another, and in less than a second, he had gone back seventeen years to the day Amanda had made her first trip to the orphanage with a busload of people from the church.

She was past seventy then, but her enthusiasm had been like that of a little girl on a picnic. The songs that were sung to make the trip less monotonous had a good measure of Amanda's squeaky, off-key little voice injected into them. At the orphanage, she joined a tour of the grounds from which many younger women had to excuse themselves because of fatigue.

Amanda fell in love with one of the orphans. He was only six, towheaded, shy as a rabbit, hunching up in a corner when anyone noticed him. Anyone, that is, except Amanda. His smile spread all over his face when she looked at him.

"He reminds me so much of Paul," she said. "I see Paul that age all over again."

Oscar Carlson had seen no resemblance. Even if he could have stripped forty years from Paul, there would have been no similarity. Paul was supercilious, vain enough for five men who had done something to earn the privilege of vanity, and even at six, he had possessed little to attract affection. At that age he had earned from Oscar the only thrashing of his life. Oscar worked for Amandaa then, driving her only laundry wagon. One day Paul was seen poking a sharp stick between the horse's ribs to see how far it would go before the skin burst. Oscar was furious when he told him to stop it.

"I will if I want to," Paul had said. "My Mama owns this house. You're just a poor immigrant."

Oscar sat down on the curbing, peeled back the boy's pants, and spanked him until his screams brought Amanda to the front door of the laundry.

But at the orphanage, out of deference to Amanda, he agreed there was perhaps a likeness.

It was two days later that people began to look upon Amanda with suspicion. Their cue came from Greta Olson, wife of the grocer whom Amanda had started in business more than twenty-five years before.

"She's plain daft about that boy at the orphanage. Went back up there again yesterday, and she did. All by herself. Said she was going to adopt him. Her without a penny of her own. She knows they don't put kids out to people her age. Crazy, I think. Of course, it's easy to see why she's so taken—she never got any satisfaction out of her own."

Oscar Carlson reflected upon that as the preacher began his eulogy.

Paul had learned only how to receive. He was a magnetic pole to which all pleasures should flow. He knew nothing of the first years of his life, except that his mother was always busy. His father died before he was born. Amanda had told him that, but not that she had scrubbed the tile floors of the Midland Hoel for a living before he came. Nor that she had taken in washings to support him, using a wooden scrub board and heating flatirons on an old coal stove. Nor that she had denied him nothing while she skimped and saved so that by the time he was six she could open a small but well-equipped laundry in order to further the enrichment of his life.

Nor had she ever told him that in spite of her frugality, she had found the means to answer the appeal of her countrymen who wished to share the abundant American life.

Oscar had been the third of the "poor immigrates." He had offered to work out his debt to Amanda, but she insisted that he accept regular wages.

"There's time enough to pay when you're on your feet."

She repeated this to many others, many of whom never realized when they had finally gotten on their feet.

Paul never had found his feet. Sixty-three he was, and not even experimentally had he tried to use the feet Amanda had formed for him. When he was twelve, the summer before he went away to military school, Amanda sent him to deliver a bundle of laundry that had not been ready when the delivery wagon left. To do so, he had to cross the river, and when he reached the middle of the bridge, he stopped and looked down into the sluggish water. The next morning, she called him before the irate customer who had come in to complain.

"Where did you take Mr. Patterson's laundry, Paul?"

"Nowhere," he answered, without guile or shame. "I just threw it in the river to see if it would float."

In 1918, he was drafted into the infantry, a blow his vanity could not sustain. The world was a war, but not Paul's world. What was he to gain by the conflict of fools? He told Amanda, after he was in uniform, that he could enter officer's training school if he could provide a bond of two thousand dollars. Amanda never questioned the logic of this, and thirty days after she sent him a check, he was at home in civilian clothes.

"They decided you needed me to help you." He explained to her. "The bond was forfeited, of course, but it's worth two thousand dollars to have your boy home, isn't it, Mama?"

That year, Amanda made Paul a partner in the laundry business. It had expanded rapidly, and there were six bright red trucks with gold lettering to look after, as well as all the washing and ironing. Oscar Carlson had quit his job to preserve his pride and his respect for Amanda.

While the soprano sang Rock of Ages, he thought again of the boy at the orphanage and he could hear so plainly through seventeen years the deep-hearted wish in Amanda's words, "I see Paul that age all over again." The words of a mind giving unction to a heart wounded by disappointment.

Paul had ruined the business within five years. He had married far out of his class, a girl named Molly Sturges, whose father had fattened his purse brokering lumber during the war. Paul may have thought he had expanded his resources, but old man Sturges knew his timber. Aside from a wedding gift of rich sterling, Paul and Molly received nothing from Sturges until he was forced to give Paul a job to save his daughter from starvation. It was Amanda who bought their house, twelve rooms of furniture, and their new car. It was Amanda who paid for clothes never worn, and who provided strawberries for a winter table. Finally, it was Amanda who failed to meet the demands of her bank.

Oscar Carlson gave her all he had saved. He had not begun to make money that was later to rank him among the town's wealthiest men, and his help was ineffective.

He watched the soprano's mouth as she sang. It was Greta Olson's mouth. She sang well for a grocer's wife; that is, she sang in key, and her notes were round, but the Rock of Ages, it seemed to him, was cold. He wondered if she was remembering the day after Amanda's third trip to the orphanage.

"Plain crazy," was what the mouth had said then. "Listen to what she told them at the orphanage. She said, mind you, she wanted to adopt the boy for Paul and his wife. Imagine. Everybody knows they can't stand kids. Just imagine such a crazy thing. They're getting used to her at the orphanage. Told her an adoption would cost too much for her. Crazy, gosh!"

The words she sang sounded the same as the words she had spoken.

That anyone could think Amanda crazy angered Oscar. She had only tried to follow Paul into his world. The path she sought was strange to the Greta Olsons, and the mind that led her was wearied by the search. But far from mad.

A year went by before she returned to the orphanage for the fourth time. Staying alone in the small church-owned house, she devoted herself to caring for the sick and helpless. She crafted gifts such as crocheted shoes for newborns and linen dust caps for women who hadn't worn such items in twenty years.

Amanda saw Paul that year only when she went to his home with a gift she had fashioned with her own hands. At Easter time, she took him a pot of paper tulips planted in the earth. She had filled a dozen other pots and carried them, two at a time, to brighten the rooms of the hospital. Paul scolded her. He told her that he was becoming embarrassed by her conduct. She was hurt for a while; then, she would try again to reach him.

Oscar thought of the morning he went to her house with a basket of groceries, using the back door because he always left his basket on the kitchen table so Amanda would think, when she discovered it, that it was something she had ordered herself. He found her sitting by the front room window from which the crocheted curtains had been removed. Her small lap was full of curtains, and the floor surrounding her chair was covered by ravelings.

Oscar had watched her for a moment as her swift; nimble fingers pulled the curtains into nothing but long, curly threads.

"Just the material I need, Oscar," she said, smiling up at him. "I'm going to make a spread for Paul's boy's bed. They're getting him a new one. The other is so small. He's almost seven now, you know."

Her hands worked feverishly, as if she were intent upon finishing the spread that day.

"You'll never stop doing for Paul, will you, Amanda," Oscar had said, thinking what Greta Olson would make of this he was witnessing. She and the others had made so much of the tulip incident, and there was a great deal of talk, and Paul had said he guessed it was time he "did something about Mama."

Nothing was done until after Amanda's last trip to the orphanage. She sat before the superintendent's desk, patting a bulging purse she held on her knee.

I won't bother you anymore," she said delightedly. "This time, I've brought all the money that's needed for my boy.

She opened her purse and withdrew four packages of her money, a hundred pieces of rectangular paper colored with green crayon.

Greta Olson sang her last "Let me hide myself in Thee," and there was abrupt silence. Dr. Samuels, who had attended Amanda, coughed, and Oscar looked toward him.

"There was nothing else to be done," Dr. Samuels had told him the day Paul had asked him to verify his testimony to the county court that his mother should be committed to the county home.

Oscar had replied heatedly: "Well, there is. I'm not going to let that son of hers poke her into a hole just to get rid of her. He's afraid he's going to have to keep her in one of those twelve empty rooms in his house."

He had gone at once to Paul's lawyer.

What Paul does to himself is none of my business," he had said. "But what he does to Amanda is. There's only a small part of her in Paul. A lot of her is in me and everybody else in this town— everybody who ever needed love and kindness and affection and money has mortgaged his heart to Amanda Pearson. I have a big house. Why can't Amanda spend her few remaining days there in comfort and happiness?

It was for Paul to decide, the lawyer had replied.

"I never question the honor of a court," said Oscar. "But it's hard for me to rest Amanda's fate in Paul's hands. God certainly wouldn't."

"She lived in Oscar's house for more than fifteen years. Paul rarely visited her. He came on Christmas alone, and stayed no longer than Amanda held him with her questions, personal little interrogations that annoyed him. She was eternally inquiring about his boy, and each time; he assured her the boy existed only in her imagination. He thought he was convincing, but on the next visit, the boy was quite as real to her as he ever had been.

Oscar had kept in touch with the orphanage, and sent gifts to the boy there, gifts a mother would send a growing son. Always, they were from "Mother Pearson." When the boy was twelve, he began writing her letters, which she cherished, and her answers always were to her "Dear Son."

Oscar brought him to the house for occasional weekends during the summer. No matter in what way Amanda's mind failed her at other times she remembered distinctly every detail of the boy's previous visit. When he was seventeen, the year before he left for college, he came bearing his first gift—a small lamp he had crafted himself.

Amanda was overwhelmed. Paul had brought her gifts, store-bought, store-wrapped, but the lamp, with marks of over-polish and clumsily concealed mistakes, made with thoughts, a heart, and with hands for her, was her first real gift.

"For me," she said when she could find her voice. "For me."

With one arm, she hugged the lamp to her breast; with the other, she drew the boy's face down to hers and kissed it.

"Son, you've made me so very, very happy."

After that she never referred to him by any name but Paul.

One morning, she called Oscar to her room. She sat in a rocking-chair near a window overlooking the front lawn. Her eyes were as bright as the green of the dew-tipped grass.

"This is a lovely house, Oscar," she said. "I'll not like leaving it."

"You're not going to leave it, Amanda," he told her.

She smiled. "Yes, I am. Soon. I'm going to die, Oscar. I want to leave this house to Paul. He needs the room for his children. Do you think he will live in it, Oscar?"

"Why—yes, I guess so. Why shouldn't he, Amanda?"

"He's so young, and everything's so new to him and his little wife from the East. Maybe they'll think the house too big, too old, Oscar."

She looked out the window for a long time. Then she said to Oscar, without facing him, "Will you have Mr. Richmond come in to see me?"

Mr. Richmond had been her attorney years before, and had died shortly after her business collapsed.

"If Mr. Richmond can't come, will Mr. Peters be able to help you?" Oscar had said.

"Why, I suppose so. If you think he's all right, Oscar."

The next morning, she did not get out of bed. Dr. Samuels came, and he told Oscar that she would never move from it again. She asked repeatedly for Paul. Oscar sent for Paul, her son, and when he came into the room, she opened her eyes and smiled at him.

"Mr. Richmond," she said scarcely above a whisper. "I'm glad you could come instead of Mr. Peters."

She closed her eyes and remained still for several minutes. Then, without opening them, she said, "Have someone sing Rock of

Ages." She was silent again." And I'd like organ music—sweet, soft organ music."

The organ was playing softly now, and coughs erupted here and there, and white handkerchiefs fluttered to faces. Oscar held his breath to keep the tears from rolling out of his eyes. He looked at Paul in the mourner's pew, and at Molly sitting beside him, her face expressionless as a wooden salad bowl. It was time for everyone to pass before the casket, and suddenly, Paul lowered his face to his hands. It was his mother he was to bury, and here he sat with nothing from her but the identity of a man long dead. All her love belonged to the boy behind Oscar Carlson in the procession.

And when the boy reached the casket, he stopped and looked upon the satin face, and he said softly, tenderly, "God bless you, Mother."

The End

The Solid Citizen

By Raymond Johnson

Artie Nelson was in a ward at city Hospital. The two cops knew he was sick and that his belly hurt, but they kept pushing questions at him and trying to make him say what he didn't mean. Artie's one eye was bloodshot with the pain and the fever of shock, and the slit made by the lid over the hole where his other eye had been looked like a misplaced streak of lipstick.

Despite Artie being physically unattractive, the clean white sheet on his bed, the spotless white pillowcase, and the neatly folded smooth white counterpane over his chest lent him a handsome appearance. In spite of his pain, in spite of the fact that the clock that Frankie Marcelino had brought would not assure him of another dawn, Artie was richer in his sanctuary than he ever had been in his life.

For Artie knew an important thing. It was a little thing to the press, a little horrible thing to that crowd of people on the corner near Feinstein's drug store, a hideous, brutal thing to society, but to Artie, it was as important as the color of leaves in October, as important as the smell of the soil in the farmer's fields at plowing time, as important as the warmth of the womb during gestation. It was something Artie felt, without knowing why, the press could not report, the little crowd of spectators could not understand, something the mass mind of society could only lose in the lifeless zone of compiled data.

The cops could ask questions until the moon turned pink and they would never know more than that muscles had moved savagely and voices had intoned shrilly a violent demonstration of the unchangeable littleness of man.

But to Artie, it was important that Frankie Marcelino was free and that he had not lost all the three hundred dollars he had saved toward a trip to the Philippine Islands.

"You got a girl in the Islands?" Artie had asked him.

"Sure, sure," Frankie answered in that singy way Filipinos talk when their enthusiasm mounts. "In Manila. Five years since I see her."

"That's a long time and a hell of a long way," Artie said.

"Seven thousand miles," Frankie said. "Long way. Long way to make love." Then he laughed as if he thought it very, very funny.

"Don't you go for these white dames here?" said Artie.

"Oh—some," Frankie said as if doubting the wisdom of answering. Then, more confident of Artie, he held up an index finger. "One. She is beautiful. I like her very much."

"Is she the marrying kind, or does she –ah—"

Frankie giggled with embarrassment and turned his eyes away. "No, no.

She very good girl."

They had been together less than ten minutes, Artie and Frankie, but their friendship had developed into a mutual feeling of trust. The land's width offered few friends to Artie, and among the men of white skin, the brown man commands only the respect of a servant.

It was past midnight when Artie hit town, and the first thing he did was walk into Poofy's Café and ask for food. Frankie was a nightman, and he worked alone.

"Sure, I'll feed you," said Frankie, and his face seemed all teeth as he smiled. That is the way Filipinos talk, with a smile. Some of them use gestures, but most do not. Their ardor, their passion, and their enthusiasm are in their voices, their eyes, and their mouths, and profoundly sincere.

Artie talked, and Frankie talked and smiled or laughed at something Artie said. Their friendship grew by the minute. Frankie's amazement over Artie's size was undiminishing. Artie was not tremendous, but sitting at the greasy, crumb-coated counter, he was monolithic in the eyes of the little man.

In their talk there were a few things Artie did not tell Frankie. He had come up from Eagle City to find a job. This he told. But he did not say that he also wished to find a girl to pose as his sister in the records of his parole status. His own sister lived in Phoenix, and since she had gone through high school, acquiring for herself a degree of learning unprecedented in Artie's family, she always had considered Artie a bum.

A parolee cannot move about with ease unless he makes the acquaintance of Mr. Fix, as Artie did. Mr. Fix had told Artie it was easy to find a woman in Baldwin City who would act as your wife, your sister, or your mother for twenty or thirty dollars. This information was free. Ordinarily the advice of a Mr. Fix comes high, for his clients usually are those in a position to lay heavy grease in the proper palm. In Eagle City, Artie's Mr. Fix was known as Baldy Collins, and according to Artie, Baldy Collins had a complete catalog of parole agents in the country who could be reached through the crisp whisper of cash.

This Artie told the cops later, but he said nothing about it to Frankie.

"Maybe Frankie wouldn't understand," Artie said to himself as he took off his clothes to go to bed.

Frankie's cup of generosity was a large one. After feeding Artie six eggs, eight slices of toast, and an unaccounted quantity of coffee, he gave Artie the key to his room.

"He's a genoo-ine good kid." He looked at his dusty face in the speckled mirror on Frankie's closet door. He rubbed his brushy chin. "Genoo-ine. What the hell does he care how many eyes a guy's got or what kind of nose."

Artie was not a criminal. Although he tended to seek the path of least resistance, he never harbored any intent to do harm. The night he heard that his mother had died, the only thought that entered his head was getting home in time for her funeral. He took a parked car and was within twenty miles of home when it ran out of gas. After the funeral, he borrowed two dollars from Steve Larkins, who ran a laundry in his hometown, bought a can of gas, and went back to get the car. The car was gone, but the principle behind its disappearance in the first place was not. For some reason—Artie often wondered if the judge had resented that one blue eye boring into him – he received the maximum penalty.

"I'll tell Frankie after I get a job," he mumbled into his hands as he scrubbed his face. "A guy workin' doesn't seem so much like a bum."

When Artie found trouble locating a job Frankie took him down to Feinstein's drug store, less than a block from Poofy's. Feinstein gave him the job—washing windows, mopping floors, dusting merchandise, scrubbing the soda fountain, and after Feinstein closed up for the night, he was supposed to come back to sweep up and see that the night lights were burning.

"Twenty-five bucks a week," said Feinstein, and to Artie, it was a magnificent sum.

While they were there, two girls came into the store. Frankie forgot Artie. He went over to the little one, lighted up his teeth in a big smile, and took off his hat.

Frankie called the girl Birdie. She was cute, not over eighteen, but to Artie, her glitter was brass. She knew her way around better than Frankie thought. She gave Frankie a phony smile, and the two left the store arm-in-arm. The other girl, Birdie's sister, a crusty-looking blonde with eyes that spoke of sinusitis and sodium barbital, remained at the soda fountain to smear grease from her crimson lips on a coffee cup.

Artie's first job was to get up on a stepladder and wash the big plate-glass windows that wore a heavy coat of grime. It was a shaky business for a man, Artie's size, to lean on two hundred square feet of glass that was held by nothing but termite-ridden wood and some tin strips with half the screws missing.

After Artie finished the windows, he went behind the fountain to clean its sink. The girl remained seated, chatting with Feinstein. Once Feinstein departed, she turned her attention to Artie.

"My name's Jean Finch," she said. "You're new here, but I've seen you around Poofy's with Frankie. Where you from?"

"Eagle City," he said, without looking up.

"Well," she said. "I know some people there. Quite a few. Ever hear of Baldy Collins?"

Artie looked straight at her with his one eye.

"Never heard of him in my life."

"Well," she said, and that was all.

After supper Artie found out from Feinstein where Jean lived and went over to see her. She and Birdie had a small apartment in a dirty red-brick building a couple of blocks from Feinstein's. The apartment was nothing like the outside of the building. Crowded with furniture and bric-a-brac, it had the appearance of easy credit or ready cash. As dogs come to resemble their masters, apartments likewise favor their occupants. Anywhere in the world, this apartment, with all its French dolls crowded against fluffy pillows, and its brassy hangover atmosphere, could be identified as that of Jean and Birdie Finch.

Jean removed a doll from a chair so Artie could sit down.

"I thought you'd be here," she said. "Like a drink?"

Artie shook his head. "How did you guess?"

"I know a few symptoms," said Jean.

"I didn't want to say anything Feinstein would hear. I've got to keep that job."

"Baldy Collins and I have known each other a long time," she said. "We've done a little business together. What's yours?"

"Nothing serious," said Artie. "All I need's a sister and an address to keep the parole board happy."

It can be arranged," said Jean.

"How much?"

"Fifty."

"Baldy said maybe twenty or thirty."

"Things run higher these days," she said. "My price is fifty. You see, I've got to do a little fixing myself."

Fifty dollars was a lot of money to Artie. It meant a three-week wait for money of his own, three weeks of sponging Frankie's generosity.

"Ok," he said. "How much time have I got?"

"Tomorrow morning," said Jean.

"I haven't got it. Not a dime to my name."

"Maybe you can get it."

"Where?"

"That's not my problem," she said, and she drained her glass. "Sure you won't have a beer?"

Before Artie left, Birdie came home. She brought a big, sober-faced bundle with her that Jean introduced as Al Gruber. Artie had seen him once at Poofy's, and had pegged him as a quiet cop who had a general dislike for humanity. He tried to figure out how Gruber and Birdie fit together, and after they sat down in the divan, he knew why the smile Birdie had given Frankie was phony.

Artie left and walked over to Poofy's. He was bothered by the Gruber-Birdie setup, but more by Jean Finch's big steal. There was no time to look for better terms. Maybe Frankie would have an idea.

"I got some bad news today," he said when Frankie set a plate of hot cakes before him.

Frankie got a sad look on his face.

This is rotten, thought Artie. "My sis needs fifty bucks right away, and I'm so flat I could slide into a slot machine."

"You got a job," Frankie said.

"I can't ask Feinstein for two weeks in advance. He thinks I'm a floater."

"You pay back little each week," said Frankie. "Like when you buy a watch."

"I never bought a watch," said Artie.

Frankie laughed. "I got fifty dollars left."

"No," said Artie. "No, Frankie, I couldn't take your money."

"Sure," said Frankie. "Sometimes, I lend money to Filipino boys. They pay back little each week."

Artie let Frankie put in the effort to cheer him up for his sister's sake, and eventually, he agreed to accept the money.

When a customer came in, Frankie attended to them. By the time Frankie was done, Artie had finished the hotcakes.

"You think a lot of this Birdie Finch?" said Artie. "You like her as much as you did the other night?"

Frankie's face was full of teeth again. "Oh, sure. More."

He dug his hands into his pants pocket and removed a small jewelry box. It held a diamond as big as a pencil eraser.

"Very, very much more," he said.

Artie's lone eye tried hard to remain normal.

"By God, you must. Think she'll take it?"

"Sure, sure," said Frankie. "She picked it out today."

"You giving it to her for fun, or is she going to marry you?"

Frankie looked uncertain. "I think she will marry me. She says maybe."

"How does this guy Gruber figure in?" Artie said abruptly.

Frankie snapped the box shut. "He no good. All the time, try to make Birdie his girl. He gets mad at her because she likes me. She all the time chases him away."

"Yeah," said Artie. "I think I know what you mean."

The next morning, Artie was cleaning out the stockroom of Feinstein's store when Al Gruber entered through the rear door. Gruber gave him a nod and sat down on a case of tissue paper. He took a penknife from his pocket and began cleaning his fingernails.

"Jean Finch told me why you went to see her last night," he said, without raising his eyes.

Artie stopped sweeping and waited.

"Eagle City, huh?" said Gruber.

"Don't waste time," said Artie. "What's the pitch?"

"Little matter of keeping parole," said Gruber. "You know you've already broken twice, don't you?"

"What's it to you?" said Artie.

Gruber closed his knife and looked up. "I'm in the business. I'm your parole agent."

Artie's throat felt gummy. "So that's how Jean tagged me. Well, I walked in with both feet."

"There's nothing to be excited about – yet," said Gruber.

"Don't forget Jean has a little—say, professional fee – coming to her," Gruber said.

"She'll get it."

"Another thing," said Gruber, lighting a cigarette.

"Feinstein has a rabid dislike for ex-cons. He's been held up half a dozen times in the past two years. Terribly prejudiced."

He stood up, and stepped closer to Artie. "The next time, Feinstein might think it was you. For a small sum – like five bucks a week—"

"I don't think you've got the guts," Artie sneered.

Gruber brushed him and went over to the door that led to the front of the store. "Let's be more discreet in our choice of words," he said, then he went up to the soda fountain and sat down.

Artie knew Gruber had guts enough to do anything for his own hide. He had eyes like grey iron, cold and unfeeling and too hard to see behind. Hid were the eyes that searched beneath the rot of cities, and his was the will of Birdie Finch.

Artie was trying to figure out how Frankie fit into their setup when Frankie came in with the fifty dollars he needed for Jean.

"Frankie," he said, "I've got a bad feeling about that diamond. Hold it a while. Let Birdie beg for it."

"I gave it to her this morning," Frankie said. "She bawls like a baby. She so happy. Why you feel bad?"

"I thought maybe she'd – lose it. Maybe I'm wrong. Thanks for the fifty, Frankie. I'll give you ten of it Saturday, like we agreed."

Gruber was in and out of the store all week. He came in every morning for coffee. Twice, Birdie was with him. She was wearing Frankie's ring –three hundred dollars' worth of greasy night-hashing and a two-by-four room in a dirty rooming-house. Artie felt the urge to clip her lightly on the chin.

Saturday was payday, and Gruber came in just before Feinstein paid Artie. He sat down and waited, then called Artie over to the fountain.

"Sit down," he said.

"I'm in a hurry," Artie told him.

"This won't take long. I seem to remember a little arrangement we made in the back room."

"You did the talking," Artie said. "I didn't say anything I had to remember."

Gruber's lips cracked open on one side, and he talked through his teeth.

"Evidently, there were a few things Baldy Collins didn't tell you."

Artie's eye was fiercely defiant. "There was a hell of a lot of things he didn't have to tell me."

Artie exited the store and headed to Poofy's. It was still too early to catch Frankie, so he took a seat at the counter and ordered dinner. Al Gruber and Birdie pestered him so relentlessly that he couldn't eat in peace. Together, they were trimming Frankie down, and they were not being neat about it.

As he was about to leave, Birdie came in alone. She sat down in a booth across the room. Artie waited until her order came, then went over and sat down opposite her.

"Hello," Birdie said in her syrupy way. She turned on one of her phony smiles.

"Cut out the good cheer," Artie said. "I'm going to hit low."

"What on earth do you mean?" she said with unripe indignation.

"What are you trying to do to Frankie Marcelino?"

She stole a haughty air from a Bette Davis movie. "I don't know what you're talking about. My personal affairs are none of your business."

"They are if they include Frankie," said Artie. "I happen to like the kid. Why don't you give back his ring before it gets you in trouble."

She began wrinkling up her nose, quivering her lips, and forcing tears from her eyes.

"Save your fake sobs for when Al Gruber takes the ring away from you," Artie said and left.

Late that night Gruber came to Frankie's room as Artie was about to go to bed.

"Listen here, stuff," he said. "I don't like having fourth-rate punks trying to make a fool of me. You went a little too far with Birdie."

Artie got off the bed and took a few steps toward him.

"I knew what I was doing, Gruber."

"Maybe I'd better refresh your memory," Gruber said. "You're the guy on parole, not me, but what if he got hold of some records of yours he doesn't have?" The lids on his eyes lowered a little. "And by God, anywhere you go, I can make you beg for a living."

Artie backed down.

"Get out of here, Gruber."

"From now on," Gruber said, "that five bucks a week will be ten."

"Get out of here, Gruber."

Gruber dogged him all week. Never before had Artie got so sick of another man's face. He knew it could not go on. Either he would weaken and fade out, or he would have to find a way to back Gruber against the wall. He wanted to keep Frankie from being hurt, but you can't tell a boy like Frankie his girl is making a monkey of him. When Frankie gave out for a girl, he gave heart and soul as well as cash.

When Feinstein paid Artie Saturday night, Gruber followed him over to Poofy's. He sat down on the stool next to his.

"Remember our little party last week?" he said quietly. "Quit stalling, mug; you can't keep it up."

"Look, Gruber," said Artie. "How much will it take to make you forget me and to get Frankie's ring back."

"You don't make sense," said Gruber.

"I'm talking your language," said Artie. "Frankie had some money you wanted. Birdie couldn't get cash so you let her take the next best. I don't give a damn what you do to Birdie, but I care a hell of a lot what happens to Frankie."

"Your heads in a marijuana haze," said Gruber. "But to set you straight – when I play games, I play them my way. Now, how about the ten."

Artie looked at him so hard his one eye hurt with hate.

"I can play games, too, Gruber," he said. "I'm keeping the ten. You make the next move."

Gruber did.

On Monday night, Jean notified Artie that Gruber wanted to meet him at her place. However, Gruber didn't show up. Jean kept Artie waiting until he was an hour overdue for checking Feinstein's lights and sweeping up.

When he reached the store he found the bars over the back door had been cut and the lock pried off. Feinstein kept no money in the store, but the liquor closet had been broken open, and four cases of whiskey were missing. Artie checked the showcases in front. All six cameras were gone, fourteen fountain pens and sixteen flashlights.

Gruber had done a good job. Here was this punk from Eagle City with a theft record. He had Feinstein's confidence, and any cop would know he had broken the locks and cut the bars to divert suspicion. Unless Artie was badly mistaken about Gruber, the missing merchandise was in Frankie's room.

"That's how it stacks, Artie," he told himself.

Gruber had him down, and he couldn't even yell.

He ran over to Poofy's.

"Why you run?" said Frankie. "What happen?"

"I've got to lam out of here quick," said Artie.

"Your sister?"

Artie shook his head.

"Feinstein's been robbed, and I'm ripe to be picked for the job. I didn't do it, but my word hasn't been worth a damn since a year ago last Thursday. You've been a real pal, Frankie, and I won't let you down. I'll send the thirty bucks I still owe you."

He told Frankie about Gruber and Jean, about the stolen car, and Eagle City. He was talking too fast. Frankie only stood there with a stunned look on his face.

"I swear, Frankie, I won't let you down."

"Maybe we go to the police?" said Frankie.

"Oh hell, Frankie!"

"What I can do to help?"

"You've got a job of your own," said Artie. "Get your ring back from Birdie. Get it before it's gone for good."

Frankie looked at him like a boy with sad news from home.

"I hate to give it to you like this," said Artie, "but I don't have time to play. Al Gruber's working that kid for all her phony little smiles is worth it. She'll give you the air, Gruber takes the ring, and you kiss three hundred bucks goodbye. Believe me, Frankie."

Artie was cutting him up inside, this flat-nosed, brown-faced little guy whose love talked with all he had. His eyes got misty, and his thick lips trembled. He was feeling the combat of love, betrayal, and a smoke-thin faith in a one-eyed man. Then fury took over, and the smile that revealed his teeth went back several generations to the savage hate of Luzon hills.

"Gruber," he said.

He picked up the narrow bun knife beside the griddle, stared at its thin, pointed blade, and fixed the handle firmly in his fingers.

"Don't be a sap," said Artie. "That's kid stuff."

Frankie did not hear. He darted past him and through the door, leaving Poofy's dim diner naked and unprotected. He was like a humming-bird swift in the evening.

"Frankie," Artie shouted after him.

By the time he reached the street Frankie was at the Alley. He turned into it and vanished in its thick, dirty shadows. When Artie reached the alley he could hear his rapid feet grinding the cinders at the other end.

"Frankie!"

The name was a shrill cry as it pierced the dead morning silence of the hollow alley.

Artie swore at himself for telling Frankie about Gruber and Birdie. The kid and his knife were out for a bigger package than the ring was worth.

He ran all the way over to Birdie's apartment, his one eye too slow in the dark to keep him from stumbling over curbings that weren't seen and those that were seen but had no form. There was no one at the apartment. He went back to Poofy's. A drunk was at the counter, his head pillowed on folded arms, but Frankie was not there.

Artie's time was running out. Before long, Feinstein's robbery would be reported and Artie still would be playing tag along the shabby streets in front of Poofy's Café. He would leave Frankie to do what he would. Whatever violence befell Gruber and Birdie would be less than they should have.

He turned back toward Feinstein's corner, and there was Frankie standing on the sidewalk, his white apron waving placidly in the breeze in contrast to the raging beat of his heart. His fist was against his belly, the knife projecting twelve inches in front of him. In the shadows of the doorway was Al Gruber, pressing himself flat as he could against the door.

"Get that idiot away from here," said Gruber with a chill of terror.

Artie cautiously approached the Filipino.

"Frankie."

Not a word was spoken by the boy's mouth, but the tenseness of his muscles wildly spoke.

"He's not worth what you're doing to your neck," said Artie.

Still, Frankie did not relax.

"I'm not smart enough to talk you out of this, Frankie. I'll have to hurt you to do it."

He leaped forward, reaching for the knife. A small fist with a trigger spring shot into his belly. Frankie moved slowly toward

Gruber. Artie swung his hand and cut him across the nape of the neck. The blow stunned Frankie; he dropped the knife. Gruber's right foot shot up and split the skin of his chin.

A crowd was forming. No matter how deeply humanity slept, the smell of suffering flesh drew people out in a curious cluster. It wouldn't be long before the police arrived.

Gruber darted from the doorway as Frankie slumped. Artie swung a glancing blow that scraped his ear. Gruber tried a kick between Artie's legs, but he was out of reach. Artie rushed in and smashed a fist hard against his nose. He fell back against Feinstein's window. It rattled like marbles in a barrel. Gruber recovered and lunged toward Artie, but he smacked into a terrific haymaker. Gruber doubled, fell butt flat against the window. The glass split.

Artie crowded him and took a stinger on the chin that was blinding. He went back, sank his fingers into Gruber's throat, and pounded his head against the plate glass. A hundred other cracks appeared, and big, ragged chunks of glass began falling, filling the night with the brittle agony of a million violent shards. Gruber pushed Artie back just as a ten-pound sliver, the shape of an icicle, pierced his neck. His throaty sobbing scream was reiterated in pinched shrieks from women in the crowd.

Artie slipped on the glass-strewn sidewalk, stumbled over Gruber's scrambling form, and another sliver followed its mate, burying its nose deep in his belly.

The next thing he knew he was in a clean bed, and his body felt clean, and there was a clean smell in the ward despite the dozen other men. Except for the pain under the wrappings of his body, he felt as he did so long ago when Mom tucked the covers tight about his shoulders.

"That Frankie," he said, looking at his clock.

Frankie had to bring him something, and no one but Frankie would think of bringing a dying man a clock. It was not a cheap, rattly clock, but a silent thing with a gentle brown face. It was a beautiful clock. Time never had been of importance to Artie, now it was of the least, but the clock had a meaning that transcended time.

Artie's pains were worse when the cops came in and pumped him dry.

"Why did you want to kill Gruber?"

"You tried to break that glass with Gruber's head, didn't you?

"You wanted to kill Gruber. Why?

He had answered their questions once, but they had not heard the important thing.

He looked at the clock.

The End

The Hut of the Blind Old Man

Raymond Johnson

John Gaines, standing in the doorway and facing the darkness of the forest across the river, knew when he sent Aimee back to town with her brother Mark that afternoon, he renounced everything that had any real significance to him. He stood alone with his greatness. He wanted Aimee. He wanted Angie and Amilee, whose faint sobs he heard continually in the rippling of Singing River which flowed before his house.

At the last moment, while Mark was waiting for her in the car up on the road, Aimee stood before him and said, "Isn't there something I can do, John? Anything?

Anything… During that moment of silence which held them apart he pondered that word.

He wanted to say, "Yes, there is. Wait one more minute, Aimee, I'll know that I can't resist you, that what I am doing is vain and foolish."

But he had said nothing, and she did not wait, and if Mrs. McPherson had not come in, he would have gone to the racks that filled one end of the room and torn to shreds every doll that filled them.

"He was a pretty lady, that one," Mrs. McPherson said. "She seemed so taken with our garden."

"But it is October."

"Well, the chrysanthemums is fresh, an' the roses is bloomin' their fool selves to death. She looked like she belongs to 'em."

He answered Mrs. McPherson. "Maybe she does. The frosts haven't killed yet."

Mrs. McPherson understood very little of what he said to her. She understood very little of what he did. In the village where she lived, a hidden corner of the valley where thoughts were old and knowledge was but remembrance, he had the reputation of being a "queer one."

Every day, she arrived to sew costumes for the dolls he had crafted the previous night. In the evening, she returned to prepare his dinner and pack his basket for the next day. She arranged the dolls by their costume colors: blue on the left, red on the right, green nestled against the basket beside him, and yellow at the farthest end. He had made this a rule that must not be broken. She talked incessantly and was forever probing into his past. He told her nothing. He never asked what circumstances she was in, but she seemed glad to receive the little he was able to pay her. She was charitable, she told him. Not once but a hundred times, she reminded him that she was charitable. And out of charity, she made her son Davie drive him to the city every morning in his stormy jalopy.

Mrs. McPherson was never quite sure whether he was blind or merely pretended blindness in order to make it easier for him to sell his dolls on the city streets. He sensed her watching him, waiting for a mistake that would betray him. Even as she worked with him, she was never certain that everything he saw about the dolls, about the bouquets of flowers he tied together and sold during the summer, he saw with his hands.

It was only during the past year that he had a need for Mrs. McPherson. When he first came to Singing River, he was able to watch its waters flow brightly before his house, and at night, the shallow, rocky stream tossed the light of the moon against his windows with a thousand tiny tumbling mirrors.

Every evening, he stood in the doorway of his house and watched the gray cloak of darkness draw about the forest beyond the river. There was a gradual diminution of detail, of slowly fading outlines, and the shadows grew heavier but were still definitely shadows of the tremendous mass of blackness behind them. Above the black ran a line of division of forest and sky, and above the line was a span of grey he came to know as the sky. The river before it all became but a shimmering movement, not describable as light yet not entirely unseen. For three years, he watched these, knowing that ultimately, they would become the same mass, blending so slowly he would be scarcely aware of the mixture.

When it was achieved, more abruptly than he had expected, he knew no sensation of fright, no panic. Instead, he felt pride and relief, as if the moment had signaled his readiness to accept a challenge. He had leaned heavily upon God, and every day that passed, his prayers became more vehement, for there was so much his brain and hands must learn and so little time.

"It sure doesn't look like old Snead's place," Mrs. McPherson had said when she came to work for him. She saw that he had labored fiercely to transform the wretchedness of the blind old man before him into a place of beauty.

"Snead was man an' ugly like the weeds," she said.

John had to listen to the story many times after that. Snead's neighbors gave him food and fuel year after year until finally, he went mad, and no one would go near him. Mrs. McPherson told about him not with pity or compassion, but with the sort of resentment one feels toward an intruder, and John could not help suspecting that he was regarded with the same sort of resentment.

"He ain't blind," he heard the woman tell her son. "He knows a white rose from a red one."

The irony of it made him laugh. He did not know their color. Their names and their positions had been carefully catalogued in his mind, and their scents memorized, and he had sat with them at night to learn the secrets of darkness, and the shapes of their leaves and their blossoms were their labels. For three years, he had been training his hands to feel every duty his remaining sight pointed out to them—the feel of winterkill, of mildew and rot, of insect infestation and brown wilt. He had shouted at them like an imperious master.

"You've got to know."

There is a touch of black spot on a rose leaf, and crown rot in delphinium.

"You've got to know."

Where the mulch would smother and where it would not, where to lay the straw and where the peat moss was knowledge he demanded of his hands.

Like children, sick and belabored by a tyrannical parent, they had faltered innumerable times. Their nerves had shrieked back at him furiously, "What's the use? You'll never see any of it again." In submission, he let them leave their toil. But the ego of man is quite as demanding in the part of him he cannot see as it is in the part he can, and hands returned to their work.

They had let him rejoice when Aimee and Mark came looking for the miserable shack Mark remembered, expecting to find destitution and depravity and a fierce hunger to return with them. The man and the woman would not believe it even after they had seen it, and hands laughed. But they clutched their laughter and held its bitterness and held it whole while he stood in the doorway and listened to the shoes taking blunt bits at the hard earth as they ascended the path. He heard Aimee say, "It is beautiful, Mark."

He remained in the dark doorway and listened to the woman McPherson setting his supper on the table. He wanted nothing to eat, wanted only to be alone. The woman prodded him with questions she answered herself.

"Are they kinfolks? Your kin? No, they can't be kin else they'd a been here before this. Will you let your food get cold now…?"

The little he said to her betrayed his irritability. Finally, she lifted the shrieking shield of her lantern, and struck a match to the wick; then she went slowly toward the road, the lantern handle squeaking as its rusty carrier road the encumbered motions of her rheumatic body. The sounds of her existence were lost to the sad song of the river.

In the sudden quiet, he remembered Mark saying, almost in desperation, while Aimee was beyond hearing, "You've done wonders, John, but – It's been difficult for Aimee, of course, but more so for you. You must have torn yourself to pieces. Are you sure this is right, John?"

He had practiced evasiveness. "It's always been difficult for you to understand motives, Mark. You're strictly a man of business. To you, the scheme of life is a vast network of interdependence. In a sense, you told me that once. You think for achievement, one has only to set his knowledge or skill against the square edge of convention, of standard practice, a code of ethics. If markets fluctuate, you fluctuate with them. If business goes to pot, you go to pot with it."

It was the longest speech he had given in years, and he couldn't help but laugh as he imagined how Mrs. McPherson would have reacted to such a speech.

He and Mark had spent a great deal of time together. It was during their last fishing trip when they discovered the hut beside Singing River. Leaving Aimee was only an immature thought then, an emotionalism, a young rebellion against the things he felt to be smothering him. They had wandered within sight of the shack standing dismal and forlorn behind the rank brush of the river's edge, surrounded by dense growth of undernourished birch saplings.

Fascinated, he said to Mark, "There is a place I'd like to own."

Mark followed the direction of his nod. He looked at it for a moment, then studied John for a clue to his objective. "It is undoubtedly the ugliest thing I've ever seen."

But you're only looking at the shack. Try to see it as a setting. Pull out the brush, thin the trees, remove the rock, and then look at it."

Mark laughed. "You do it... I'm taking a holiday."

He cast his line and began reeling in. Suddenly, he said, "Why on earth do you want a place like that?"

"To live in," John answered. "it's just the sort of place a man would need for rediscovering himself."

Mark looked at him. "Aimee and the girls couldn't live in a place like that."

"No," John said. "Not now."

Mark appeared to forget his line. "What's wrong, John?"

"Nothing really."

"What's this talk about a man's re-discovering himself? Has something happened between you and Aimee?"

John reeled in all the way. "Nothing, Mark. Everything I love has its beginning in Aimee, and in her, it will end. But…"

"But what?"

"Forget it."

"You started it, John."

"Mark, I'm a simple man. Aimee's sudden fame has knocked me off balance. I can't keep up with her, and I'm tremendously jealous."

"It comes easy for her, John. It isn't because she loves it more than you or the children."

"I'm sure of that, but I'm afraid – of myself. Maybe I'll get the idea she does. I don't want to. Not only because of Angie and Amilee, but because of me. I'm selfish, Mark."

"This sort of takes the slack out of me, and I don't think Aimee's ever suspected. It's time you two had a holiday together, and a good long talk with it."

There was never time for the holiday, nor for the talk. John sought it, but he never was able to select the words he needed, and when he thought he found them it seemed that he was about to choke off a part of Aimee that was quite as important as the food that sustained her.

At first, Aimee's success was both remarkable and gratifying. It pleased a man to see that his wife had qualities beyond just her hairstyle or figure that set her apart and made her even more attractive than other women.

At the bank, John already had a certain distinction of his own. It was nothing important, certainly nothing that would make him celebrate, but it was satisfying. His backyard, a small patch of city clay which he had turned with sand and cinders and leaves into good earth, had been made to produce prize-winning roses which brought him an enjoyable though confined recognition. Few people understand a man who forsakes the ordinary pastimes of men to devote his time to flower, but they will admit that accomplishing a balance in the chemistry of soil, atmosphere, and insecticides with a sense of arrangement merits some acknowledgement. Aimee made photographic studies of his garden, and their perfection focused attention upon her, and John was pleased to be known at the bank as the man with the talented wife.

Particularly so the summer before Amilee was born. A favorite study of Aimee's, to which she had tacked the rather trite title "Garden Shadows," won her an award of five hundred dollars. John was in the garden coddling a new bed for Madonna lilies when she ran out, flushed and excited and weeping, waving the check she had received.

"With this, darling, we start our family. Three. All our own. Three whole children, no more, no less."

He held her close, feeling her excitement and happiness as his own, held her for a long time, and as he was about to release her, she hugged closer to him.

"Oh, it's good, John, so good to be able to do things. It's so good to be Mrs. John Gaines."

He shared her spirit of triumph. It was good to be able to do things, a little more than simply earn a living or keep a house, to be just a little more than alive.

Amilee was their first child, and Aimee's success with pictures of her was notable. Her picture began to illustrate magazine fiction. Aimee pursued her art with incredible vitality and enthusiasm. By the time Angie was born she was working for the top advertising firms. Amilee and Angie were subjects. They were never babies. Their smiles and tears helped sell everything from matches to roofing cement. One day, John discovered that they were the most photographed children in America.

"Someday, Aimee, these girls are going to grow into awkward, freckle-faced school kids, and you won't have anything to do with them.

"John, that isn't true. They are excellent subjects. I think they always will be. And you know I'll always adore them."

"Even when you know everyone will associate them with toothpaste, laxatives, and underwear? Look here, Aimee, are you sure you want another child or – merely something new for a picture?"

She looked at him earnestly. "I'm sorry, John. I hadn't realized … Of course, I want another child, and the girls we have I want only as children – yours and mine – no one else's."

There was never another child. Perhaps, after all, it was a good thing. It could have been a boy. And after Normandy, Johns was glad he had no son to watch grow into uniform, no son he would have to make himself proud of as he shaped the uniform.

Amilee's and Angie's pictures thereafter were suitable for nothing more notorious than a family album, but Aimee was unrestrained. The freshness of her ideas, and her originality were in ever greater demand. It was never necessary for Aimee to push herself; she floated with ease. It was as if she could have gone on or stopped at will. She was simply Aimee Gaines having a lot of fun with a camera and some unusual ideas.

Then suddenly, she, as well as John, discovered that she was riding a wave that she could not control. She had become big business. She was a commodity. She had a staff of assistants, secretaries, and agents. A national magazine carried an interview with her, and Aimee Gaines became intimate with a good part of America.

"You lucky boy," said Janus Heideman, a vice president of the bank. "How does it feel to be the husband of a famous woman? And a beautiful one, too."

The inevitable banality.

"It feels like having barbed wire for breakfast," said John.

It was a childish retort, he recognized too late, and Janus disliked it.

John apologized, but more and more thereafter, he felt that he was regarded as "touchy." It was about this time that the weeds began creeping into the rose beds, and the dead wood started accumulating in the lilacs.

Then came the new house. Aimee's large, wonderful house. To everyone who had no house, or who possessed one more humble, it was a lovely dwelling. It was everybody's house. The exterior, the interior, the furnishing, the surrounding grounds – the whole damned business belonged to anyone who was addicted to magazines devoted to stripping a home of its dignity and privacy. John had unlimited earth to turn, and no longer did he have to cheat the clothing budget in order to buy a few new roots or bulbs. He had a small greenhouse for winter work, and a good shop for grafting. But his attempts at hybridizing had become strangely unsuccessful.

Everything was intolerably empty of Aimee.

One morning, John walked into Mark's office. It must have been, he thought now, that he wanted to shock him. Yes, that was it. Mark wasn't the kind of person you approached for a chat unless you were keen to discuss tax laws, dividends, capital gains, and consumer demand.

Aimee was good for Mark's business and, therefore, good for Mark, and he would get a good scare out of John's appearance alone. He had been up all night, he had been drunk, and he had not been without company.

"Good Lord!" Mark said when he saw him.

"Don't get excited," John said. "I'm not taking a dive into the gutter."

"You look shot. Do you need a drink?"

"No."

"What's happened?"

"It's an old, old theme, Mark. It would be terrible in script form."

"I don't get it, John."

"Husband and wife – wife soars to lofty heights while husband scratches gravel. The world is full of personal little calamities like that."

He put a hand on Mark's shoulder. "Don't look so worried. I've known men in my position who mixed their tears with wine and other women. Last night, I tried to find out why, and I can tell you it was the most disgusting experience of my life."

"Well, should think—"

"You're thinking of Aimee, Mark. I don't intend to disgrace her." He walked over to the window.

"But you're not that sort of man, John."

"How do you know what sort of man I am?" He walked back to Mark's side.

"Right now, I feel very mean. I want to go home and tell Aimee what I've done to try to hurt her. I know I won't. I'm afraid she'll understand and forgive me."

"Have you and Aimee ever taken that holiday?"

"We've planned it – a hundred times. It's always coming after something else, always something to look forward to."

"I feel sure, John, this whole thing can be talked out. When a business has problems, its administrators are called together to solve them. I'd insist that Aimee meet you on a business basis if on no other."

John smiled wryly. "I'm sure you would, Mark."

"You can always find a middle course," Mark said insistently.

"It's doubtful. I have the word of a lot of experts that there is. It's possible to carry two horns, but very difficult to blow them both at the same time. No human is big enough to throw the entire self into everything. The capacity simply isn't there."
"I think you're supercharging the whole business with egotism. You want Aimee to shoulder the responsibility for your – your –"

"Failure. And has there ever been a man who was delighted by the knowledge he was a failure?"

"But Aimee– "

I'm not blaming Aimee, Mark. She's a magnificent person. She's still sweet and charming as a schoolgirl. She's a part of everything I am, but she is whole without me. Good Lord, Mark, I'm a man, and I'm hungry to have her back."

Mark studied him for a moment. "You're jealous. John."

"I think I told you that once. And selfish. Remember? I used to think I had a right to be. Now, I'm not sure it's my prerogative to interfere with Aimee's great exultation. She's giving the world something it needs, although I don't understand the need. The best I can offer is a chair beside my desk in the small-loans department of a bank so customers may seat their embarrassment. Anyone with a clean shirt and a smug air can handle a job like that, but you have to look for the Aimee's."

Suddenly, Mark looked extremely worried. "Are you thinking about leaving Aimee?"

"In a sense, I have," John answered. "I'm in the army, Mark."

He thought he saw relief on Mark's face.

"A sort of boyish impulse?" Mark said as he turned away.

"No. I've thought about it a great deal. At my age, it doesn't seem smart, I know, but it prevents me from doing something – more boyish? – like packing my bags and moving to a hotel."

Mark looked at him for a moment, and then said, quite somberly, "Somehow, you don't strike me as a fighting man."

John remembered the remark, and he wondered now if Mark had and if, after what he had seen, he recognized the irony of it.

He stepped away from the open doorway, feeling the cold, damp October night air from the valley. His feet felt their way along the floor until he reached the table. He sat down, and forgetting that his supper had been placed there, his hand bumped the soup bowl. The cold, wet, and flaky grease of the soup splashed across his wrist.

Of course, he had never considered himself a man of combat. Nor had anyone else been so impressed, least of all his commanding officer, when after three days of ineptitude, he was wounded.

From a London hospital, he wrote to Aimee:

"It's scarcely worth mentioning, but if you haven't been, you will be informed that I was wounded in action. Don't be misled. It was strictly the result of inaction. Think nothing of it. Merely a nick in the head that's only severe enough to let me enjoy a little pampering."

Aimee wrote often. Her letters were hasty, but not merely dutiful. He looked forward with eagerness to letters from the girls. Amilee was ten, and her fifth-grade letters started so painstakingly. For a few lines, she wrote so precisely, so correctly, all about horses and dogs and somebody's new kittens, then as imagination took leave and impatience seized her, black erasure marks, misspelled words, and gaunt, misshapen characters filled the lines hurriedly.

"Darling Amilee, take your time, take your time…"

And Angie – he could see her pinched fingers choking her pencil, her tongue locked between her lips as she labored with her scrawl, "I love you, Daddy. My teacher is nice."

Amilee and Angie… The voice of the river…

When he was ready to be sent home, he did not tell Aimee. The doctors had told him what the effects of his wound would be. He had only to wait. He feared that whatever he told Aimee would lead to a revelation he did not know how to make.

There always would be a sanctuary. The generosity and charity of his country was tremendous. There was no sarcasm in his thought of it, but a dread. He would not be a total loss. He could be reclaimed, like old iron, poured again into a mold of something perhaps smaller but useful nevertheless. Or, that failing, someone always would take care of him, somewhere.

Aimee would do that. She was well prepared to make him a king in want of nothing. He would be warm, well-fed, entertained. He would learn to read and to do little things with his hands, so he should never know the psychological effect of utter dependence. He would be superbly provided with comforts. Perhaps a man would be hired to keep him company, to wait on him, to guide him. Thirty years – forty—maybe as many as fifty – he could dwell in complete, protected anonymity.

When he reached home that night, he could go no farther than the street. He stood there, looking at the lighted windows, with a terrible longing and desire but with a weakness that was overwhelming. He knew that once he entered the house, he would never emerge again.

"I told you that in my letter from the hotel," he said aloud, his voice husky in the timeless darkness and silence. "I tried to make you understand."

The sound of the river answered through the open door.

Aimee had hinted, just before leaving with Mark, that there had been cruelty in the letter.

"It was not meant to be," he said to the wall which held the dolls. A dozen times, I rewrote it so there would be no cruelty or a hint of self-pity. You see, then I thought I had to do what I have done."

He stood up and felt his way to the racks. He took down a doll and gripped it between his hands.

"You had created a life which suited your purpose. I had lost my purpose and created nothing. Then I remembered this miserable place, and I came here to create John Gaines."

For two years, day and night, in all manner of weather, he fought the rank brush, the rocks, the foulness of rot and dilapidation, and always in his mind was the hideous fear that he would not have time.

"But there was – just enough. Time enough to prepare me and my hands for everything except for one moment alone with you."

He listened. Beyond the sound of the river, he heard the early morning traffic heading toward the city. Morning had come so soon; it felt like just hours since Aimee had left. Her fragrance lingered in the air, and her calm, clear voice echoed in his mind. He sat down again, letting the doll fall to the floor.

"Endless. It will be endless, that moment."

Every day he was upon the city streets he had thought of its inevitability. It was a moment he knew must come, and he never let himself answer truthfully what he should do, what he should say when he met it. And when he heard Aimee and Mark coming down the path, the spasms of panic gripped him. He wanted to run and hide behind the hedge, but there was a stronger urge to yield to discovery. For a moment, a moment that crowded his conflict, he felt resentment toward Aime and Mark for coming. Then, he was thankful for Mrs. McPherson's mistake in packing his basket, for if he had not urged Angie to take a blue doll when she insisted upon a red one, she would not have called to Uncle Mark.

"And the song of the river would not be the sobs of Amilee and Angie haunting me now."

Through to the sounds of dawn, the forest waking, the sparrows upon the gutter searching the leaves for seeds, the cardinal calling a new discovery of melon seeds.

The moment was gone. He could submit to his weakness. He was a foolish man, and he could fully feel his desolation. There was no more to do than go out upon the streets with his basket. Mrs. McPherson would come soon.

"It is my life – Mrs. McPherson, my dolls, and the ghost of old Snead, the foul smell of the family aphididae plagued by the green fly."

The crust of grease had stiffened the skin of his wrist.

He had done so much; He had done nothing. He was a staggering, clumsy fool, spilling his food, colliding with fire hydrants, and stabbing his hips with cornerstones of marble. An architect can erect a tall, beautiful building. But it is meaningless in a city without people. The little bundles of flowers he sold were only a quarter's worth of wilting frailty to the people in the streets. They were not the smell and taste of soil and sand and mold and tears and sweat. And the dolls—shapes of wooden junk and cotton scraps that soon ended their empty lives in the darkness of dusty stair closets.

"Isn't there something I can do, John?"

There had not been the courage to answer, just as until yesterday, he had lacked the courage to admit that what he was doing was only a means to an undesirable end. It was the answer to the question he avoided answering: how long until he met and walked with the man who had occupied the hut before him.

Mrs. McPherson was coming. He heard her on the path. She walked lightly. It was a bad sign. She would chatter vigorously and monotonously from the moment she opened the door until her son Davie came to take him away. He wished, somehow, he could avoid her, to shut her voice out so it would not destroy what remained for Aimee.

The steps drew nearer – certainly not those of Mrs. McPherson. He dared not acknowledge their stirring familiarity. He felt brief rebellion, a conflict of impulses. He feared their reality, yet prayed urgently that they were not a delusion.

She entered slowly, uncertainly, through the open door. She was reluctant to enter, perhaps, a strange reluctance he had never sensed. It had never occurred to him that, coming to the hut, she may have felt a horrifying kinship to the blind old man.

"Are you awake, John?"

He rose to his feet.

"How could I have slept?" he said.

"You knew I would come?"

"I didn't think of your coming."

"I can't stay away, John."

"There is nothing here. You know that."

"What I saw was strong and enduring. It is what I want."

He was silent.

In an unsteady voice, he said finally, "Is there light enough to see your way closer? By the table…there. Stand there. I can touch you. I feel terribly inept and awkward."

"I love having your hand on my face, John."

There was the sound of new footsteps upon the path. Mrs. McPherson's. "John," Aimee said, in her voice was a plea. "Send her away, John, for good."

Her head rested against his chest, her arms wrapped tightly around his neck. He could hear the excitement in her breathing, and to him, it was as if the river had begun to sing a new song.

The End

Removed from the Little Man

By Raymond Johnson

George Noble was glad he had left his car at home when he went to meet Presley Edmonds. Emotionally and mentally upset, a man of fifty, a man of any age for that matter, has not the wit of a responsible driver. Besides, the long walk home would give him time to think, to unravel the conflicting thoughts that had been assaulting his mind since Presley mentioned Lynn. He needed the time to regain his composure, to examine his attitude, to destroy the resentment toward Harvey Treat which was rapidly building up in him.

There had been a certain shock of disappointment from his talk with Presley, for becoming superintendent of schools in Prairie City long had been in his heart. But this feeling withered to insignificance when he felt, with the chill of a sudden blow from an unpredicted source, the sickness of the suggestion that Harvey Treat had betrayed him.

He knew Harvey desired the job just as much as he did, maybe even more, and certainly made his ambition more obvious. Yet, it seemed inconceivable that Harvey would be willing to sacrifice a friendship that had lasted over twenty-five years. It had been a personal sacrifice of Harvey's that had brought him to Prairie City in the first place.

His thinking was still too emotional to be rational, and he knew it must be set in order before he went home to Rose. Rose was a devoted wife, but she would allow no emotionalism to influence her approach to their problems.

It was a lovely Saturday afternoon, not too hot for August, ideal for the drive he had planned to Badertown. He had promised to take Lynn over to meet Madison Guy, and his disappointment was as great as hers when Presley Edmonds called and asked him to come to his office. He was fond of Madison, and he had not been to see him for several weeks, a much too distant relationship for a prospective father-in-law to assume. But Presley Edmonds was president of the school board, and George felt his requested meeting was not merely for casual conversation.

Yet Presley had tried to make it appear casual. He was customarily rather theatrical when he talked, even in the privacy of his law office. Everything was done with a flourish. No point was made without the emphasis of a waving arm or a fist smashing into a palm. George felt the device was used more for ego assertion than for dramatic effect. At today's meeting, however, he had sat calmly behind his desk the greater part of the time, his only physical movement being a shift to a more comfortable position in his chair or to lift his cigar to his mouth.

Presley was sly. His success as a lawyer could be attributed in large measure to his ability to navigate a vast sea of apparently unimportant detail and arrive triumphantly and with startling suddenness at a port of cold, brutal fact. More often than not, this subtle maneuvering produced its effect by strong implication. The unwary was led through a maze and then abruptly was left suspended with the feeling he had escaped the wiles of his interrogator, only to realize a few seconds later, with frightening clarity, that he was bound inescapably in a web of his own making. George deplored this talent of Presley's and, unlike Harvey Treat, always avoided social relationships or frequent conversation with him.

"I've never made a point of becoming acquainted with you, Mr. Noble," Presley had said. "Personally, that is. My son helps me to understand you're quite a likable person. And your twelve successful years as principal of Clayton High speak well for you."

There was a moment of embarrassing silence. George never had known how to react to complimentary remarks. A man never reaches the age when praise becomes distasteful, nor does the modest man mature to the point of accepting it in the presence of another without discomfort.

"The board has an important meeting tonight," Pressley went on. "We have three exceptional candidates for the superintendency, one of whom should not be considered because we feel the job should go to a Prairie City man. I had you come here on my own initiative, because you are, Mr. Noble, above everyone else in the school system, in a position to help us make our decision."

He paused and looked at the lighted end of his cigar, watching the glow die as ash formed a hood over it. Then he looked up at George, hesitating a few seconds before speaking as if to test his listener's skill of anticipation.

"What, Mr. Noble, do you think of Harvey Treat?"

The direct question had a disquieting effect. It left no doubt that Harvey's tireless efforts to have himself impressed into the superintendency were about to culminate in success.

"You mean, of course, with respect to the job of superintendent," he said. He pressed his fingers together, and leaned back in the cool leather chair.

He conceded to himself that selecting Harvey would not be an unwise choice. While Harvey might be more opportunistic than aligned with his own views, there was no doubt about his qualifications as an administrator.

George felt keenly the fruitlessness of the twelve years he had spent schooling himself for the job which finally had opened, and which now would slip farther beyond reach as the years pressed upon him.

He wondered what Presley expected him to say. He could understand the motive of a man questioning an intimate about a prospective employee, but Presley Edmonds and George Noble knew each other only by reputation, far from intimately enough to discuss a matter that was strictly for the judgment of a six-member board. He felt that Presley was taking advantage of him. Whatever he said about Harvey Treat could be construed as prejudicial.

Before he said any more he thought how Harvey Treat could be disqualified easily and disastrously. Public opinion, master of men like Presley Edmonds even, especially the concerted opinion of Prairie City, could destroy Harvey Treat's ambition irrevocably. There was no danger in Harvey; it had never been, but public opinion can be made to see danger where it does not exist. But George Noble alone knew that in 1930, Harvey was a member of the Communist party.

"I have known Harvey twenty-five years," he said. "I could say nothing that would not be a recommendation."

He alerted himself to a conversational trick of Presley's. He said no more than necessary at any time, and when Presley asked a question, he paused before answering to examine its phraseology. It was more difficult to handle some of Presley's comments about Harvey. They were magnetic probes. They reached back to a point before either he or Harvey had heard of Prairie City. Presley was fencing, and George resented it.

Harvey was not brilliant. He was well-educated, but he lacked the inner passion that distinguishes a man as brilliant. There were strands in his intellect that were weak. When George first became acquainted with him, he got the impression of instability. He was inclined to go off on tangents that led nowhere. He was what one called then an intellectual faddist. He could afford to take the time to indulge in any new philosophy that raised its unripe head about the pseudo-intellectuals of the East. He would profess to be a realist and promptly begin thinking and speaking in the manner of an idealist. He had his fling with the Technocracy movement, and later, when his father was dead, and hoaxes for the depression years were tooled for mass production, he snuggled against the bosom of Communism, which, from malnutrition, he soon deserted.

These were the pieces George withheld from Presley. They were only small pieces. Harvey finally had matured safely beyond them, had established a good family and set himself earnestly to his career as a teacher. They were pieces that could, if improperly handled, instantly scramble beyond the collection of all the other pieces that Prairie City owned.

Presley held him there for three-quarters of an hour. During their conversation George detailed bits of his own background to provide light for his picture of Harvey. There was nothing intimate, yet when his visit ended, and he was about to leave, he had the feeling that Presley was in possession of more of him than he had revealed.

"How is Lynn?" Presley asked. He commented how rapidly time had passed since she and his son Douglas were graduated from high school. "I understand she's soon to be married."

Then, before George could say anything, he poised a remark which, George thought, placed him in an atmosphere of clotheslines and back fences.

"I never knew until recently that Mrs. Noble was not Lynn's mother. I've always been impressed by their resemblance."

Only he, Rose, and Harvey Treat had known this until now.

For a few seconds, before leaving Presley, he tried to reject from his mind the thought that Harvey had preceded him in a secret meeting. But the thought was obstinate and persistent, and each time it blazed up, its heat was more intense.

Had it been deliberate, or had Harvey been trapped into revealing secrets just as George was certain Presley had attempted to trap him? It was difficult to acknowledge that Harvey was contained so supremely in self that he would entirely disregard the future of three people simply to enhance his own possibilities.

He recalled that night twenty years earlier. Harvey hadn't seemed convinced at the time. His thinking had lacked discipline, and he had been somewhat skeptical about the extent of physical discipline.

There was no telling how this may affect Lynn, George thought as he turned to cross the park to save distance. He paused to admire the new planting of roses. Prairie City, these roses, were Lynn's life. The city had been good to her, generous, but not to an extravagant degree, and she loved it. Presley Edmonds may or may not retain what he knew. If the scandal of Lynn's conception were used as a factor against him, it would remain no secret to Prairie City. No matter how discreet every member of the board may be, in at least one, there would be human frailty enough to destroy the protective barrier of silence.

He reflected upon the folly of a public servant, thinking he had a secret. No matter how narrow or contemptible any segment of that public may be, he must be devoutly and wholly its servant, with no evidence of ever having borne a non-conforming standard.

Prairie City could not hurt him as Kingdom City had, but how would he protect the happiness that had filled Lynn's life and prevent the needless disruption of Roses's serenity? It would not be sufficient to say simply, "It is not true."

For Kingdom City, it had been true. Only Lynn's mother could have proved its falseness. Kingdom City, with Jane Witherow dead almost before her child was dressed, and its scandal firmly in its teeth, and nothing could shake it free.

When George first went to Kingdom City to try for a job, he found the school system wrapped in a buttonless political cloak. Harvey Treat, who had been teaching there a year, offered the only means he knew of getting inside the cloak.

"First, you must become a part of the Witherow system. Somehow, you've got to impress a Witherow."

Indeed, Witherow was a magic name. There was Witherow lumber, Witherow coal, Witherow insurance, Witherow playground equipment, Witherow banks, and he wondered if the Witherows themselves knew what else. It was an empire ruled by Thomas Witherow and his wife, Emma. Rose was their eldest daughter. She was twenty-five. Jane was only seventeen.

Rose, fortunately, came to life before the Witherow interests had consumed her parents completely, and she had a smattering of family life during her formative years. Jane, however, was expelled from warm darkness into a cold, harsh, startlingly bright world of Witherow wealth empty of affection except that provided by her sister. She had never set foot in a public school; her education was received from a procession of tutors whose understanding of the world's components had its soul in a manual of instruction.

George Noble was threadbare and hungry when he became her last teacher, the result of Harvey Treat's influence on one of Emma's friends. Trembling with self-consciousness and acute awareness of his impoverished appearance, he went for an interview at the Witherow house, an incredibly large, over-architectured structure of buff brick and terra cotta set in the middle of Witherow Park.

Emma ignored the transcripts of recommendation he carried with him.

"Jane is a born writer, so sensitive and discerning." She said. "I want you to teach her everything there is to know about composition."

It was on such an afternoon as this, he remembered, when he first saw Jane. She and Rose were coming up the ewe-hedged path from the lily pond when Emma Witherow brought him out for an introduction.

She was an attractive girl, with a slender body, her face a little too long perhaps, and her blonde hair was cut so the wind could whip it without making it appear like a tangled mop. Her eyes were large, clear, and blue, and they had in them what George thought at first was daring, impulsiveness, and determination.

The gaze she fixed upon him was so intense he had to look away.

"I'm going to enjoy your instruction very much," she said. Her words were precisely formed but spoken with a choppy effect. Then, to George's amazement, she turned to her mother and said, "At last, you've brought something warm and honest and human into our domain."

Her mother looked at her frigidly as she turned with Rose and went into the house.

During the first few weeks Jane was cooperative, but then she became restless, refusing to study, insisting that George be with her but devising all sorts of schemes to steal his attention from his work.

"You're deliberately wasting your time and my efforts," he told her one afternoon in the middle of September. He made no attempt to disguise his irritation.

They were seated on a stone bench beside the lily pond. Suddenly, she grabbed his textbook from his hands and tossed it into the water.

"Who cares about that stuffy nonsense," she cried. "I want to write about vital things, about people who move fearlessly and forcefully. I don't want my characters to sit and tat."

George was furious. He rose and pulled her to her feet. "Whatever your ultimate aim is, you'll approach it the way I tell you. Now, go get that book."

"I'll do no such thing."

He moved swiftly, impulsively, grasping both her arms and pushing her into the pond. By the time the fury of her splash had subsided, he was feeling regret, but he had gone too far to relinquish his mastery.

"Now," he ordered. "Bring that book to me."

He spent a sleepless night trying to convince himself his hasty action was justified and preparing himself for Emma Witherow's heated dismissal the next morning. But Jane, when he saw her, assured him by her attitude that any resentment she may have felt had not been expressed to her mother. Later, while he was explaining the elements of the day's assignment, she interrupted him.

"You're a fascinating person, Mr. Noble," she said. "I think you could do with me anything you wanted to."

It was not the last time she threw him off balance in that manner, and by Christmas, he realized, too late, that in him, she had objectified all the love, kindness, and generosity she had hungered for since birth.

Christmas Eve, she came to his room in the dismal rooming house where he lived. She handed him a small gift package.

"It's something I want you to have," she said. She spoke in her peculiar choppy manner, her voice quivering slightly, as if from excitement.

"You shouldn't have, Miss Witherow," he said awkwardly. He was disquieted by her gift

as much as by her visit. "You really shouldn't have."

"Why not?" she demanded. "At Christmas, people give presents because it's the customary thing to do – why can't they do it because they want to?"

"A token maybe, but this—I have a feeling this is not merely a token, Miss Witherow."

"Miss Witherow, Miss Witherow, Miss Witherow," she mocked. "Miss Witherow, if you please, requests that you open the package."

He did so clumsily. It contained an expensive watch and bracelet he would not have dared to dream of owning. The sight of it infuriated him.

"Miss Witherow, I'm sorry—" He snapped the box closed and held it out to her. "I couldn't possibly accept this from you at Christmas or at any other time."

"You could if you'd let yourself," she said, and his gesture of rejection angered her, "You should, George, but you're a fool. You're capable of crawling out of your school-teacher shell, but you're a fool."

"You're being a very silly child, Miss Witherow."

"I don't want you as a teacher any longer, George, but as a man."

"Miss Witherow, you don't realize what you're saying."

"Don't I? How can I think of something for weeks and not realize what it is when I speak of it? I love you, George Noble, with all my heart. I love you."

He grasped her firmly by the arms.

"Jane, you must go home."

"Home," she cried, and her voice became more shrill. "Home—at Christmas! Oh, how I hate that barn where I live. George—let go of me. Holding my arms like that—I can't bear it. Hold me gently—"

He released her, "Jane, you must go home to Rose. You love Rose. You wouldn't have her know you were here talking like this."

"Rose has known I've loved you ever since you came to me. You could love me, George, if you'd let yourself. You want to, but you're afraid."

He could persuade her to leave only by promising to take her home. When he returned, he met his landlady in the hall. She said nothing, but she gave him a cheerless look of disapproval, and he felt her brand of guilt follow him as he climbed the back stairs. He went to his room and immediately wrote a letter of resignation to Emma Witherow, thereby ending his hope of entering Kingdom City's school system. He ignored Emma's request for an explanation.

Jane came to his room twice after that, and each time, he felt more helpless.

"It's a situation I don't know how to manage," he confessed to Harvey Treat. "If I knew where to go, I'd take the next train out."

"Oh, come now," Harvey said. "You can't put a girl in that position and then run out on her."

"Not Jane, Harvey, I swear it."

Harvey shrugged his shoulders. "Who am I to contradict you? Well, if you really must get away, there's a place I've been fishing for in a town called Prairie City. If we handle it right, maybe, we can swing you in. But this girl sounds like a butterfly to me. Stick it out, and maybe she'll land on somebody else. Then you can forget her."

"She's too tragic to forget easily," said George. "Don't you suppose her parents have ever cared?"

"Too rich, too selfish, and too foolish," Harvey said, and then he was off on his pet subject of the day, the proletariat versus the system.

Near the end of April, Jane visited George once more. It was close to midnight, a thunderstorm had just ended, and as he was about to go to bed, she opened the door and walked in.

The sight of her astonished him. She wore a raincoat, but she was hatless, and her hair was pasted to her head and face like strands of thread. She was nervous, frightened.

"Jane—" he stammered.

"Don't scold me," she said. It was almost a plea. "I had to walk. They'd have followed if I'd come by car or cab."

"Who, Jane?"

She ignored his question.

"I had to see you. I'm going away, George."

He said nothing.

"Doesn't that mean anything to you? Coming over, I thought— If you could—Maybe a miracle would make you take me away."

"Is there something wrong? Can I help you, Jane?"

She drew closer to him as he stood up.

"Mother and father will come here looking for me. They'll never find me, George. Never. I told them it was you. I hurt you, I know, and I'm terribly, terribly sorry. I wanted it to be you so much, and I had a crazy notion you might –"

"Sit down and calm yourself," he said. "I can't understand what you're trying to tell me."

She disregarded the chair he offered. There was a hysterical sob in her throat as she spoke.

"I don't know who it was, but I've always thought of you over and over. George, I've loved you so much." She flung her arms around him and squeezed herself against him, pressing her face into his chest as she wept. "I wanted my baby to be yours, George, so much—to be yours."

A cold, spiraling sensation of fury that swept through him left a knot of sickness dangling in his stomach. He pushed the girl away, held her at arm's length, and in his anger and frustration, shook her unmercifully.

"What are you saying? What are you saying?"

Then, the sight of the pathetic object of his brutality restored his senses, and he took her compassionately in his arms.

"You pitiful, foolish child," he said. "I'll take you home."

She pulled away from him. "I'll never go back there. I'll die first. I will."

"But Jane, you must. This is something you can't—"

He saw the futility of trying to reason with her. She broke away from him, and he let her go, and with her went the story his landlady, Harvey Treat, the Witherow family, and Kingdom City should have known.

Only Rose had believed him. With courage and fierce truth, she denounced her parents and the city they had encumbered.

He and Rose left Kingdom City together after they found Jane, and a thousand miles and generous years and Lynn had a swift remedial effect.

But his walk from the office of Presley Edmonds had not, as he had hoped, remedied his attitude. He had grown uncomfortably warm as he walked, and it was no longer a lovely Saturday afternoon, but a disagreeably burdened one. He had tried to reason – primarily, he thought, to vindicate Harvey—that Presley had spoken of Lynn only in a manner of making small talk, but the argument was flimsy. There had been no necessity for it. Presley, with his remark, had tried to tell him something.

He was near home, he was not prepared to face Rose, and his bitterness toward Harvey Treat was even greater. Twenty years ago, he thought it would not matter, for he would have erected no sacred trust in Harvey.

When he reached home, Rose met him at the door. She remarked that he looked tired and suggested that he lie down before dinner. He was tired. He had not realized how tired he was until he stepped inside the cool, restful house. Rose must have guessed that he was not at peace, yet when she spoke again, it was not with apology.

"Harvey and Alice Treat are coming for dinner."

These few simple words were devastating.

"Presley Edmonds—" He blurted, then he stopped.

Anger flared in him, but it died for want of fuel. One could not look at Rose and be angry. He went to his room and lay down. And he felt the tremendous weight of his age, the fruitlessness of his work. He dreaded the coming of September.

He had no appetite at dinner, either for food or conversation. Harvey Treat, sitting beside him, apparently had no disturbing thoughts, for he filled himself with great quantities of food. The man was abnormal, George thought. If Presley Edmonds had trapped him in their conversation, he must be frightfully dense not to realize it by now. If he had been deliberate in revealing what he knew to Presley, then only colossal vanity and stupidity would allow him to exhibit his triumph with such avarice.

George watched him light his cigar after dinner. Self-satisfaction became a ritual of the process. For a moment, he wished with childish fury that he could say something to hurt Harvey. Presley Edmonds had given him the opportunity. He had been above it then. Now, he was sure that he was not.

Not for myself, he thought, not for me or the job I wanted…

The evening dragged on like a plodding horse expiring under an unbearable burden.

Rose and Alice talked, and occasionally Harvey stabbed their voices with inanities.

George pondered what had initially drawn him to Harvey and solidified their friendship. The man was neither clever nor witty and lacked any particular talent except for growing flawless roses. With enough time, patience, and a barrel of dusting powder, anyone could achieve that.

…It's for Lynn that I'm protesting. Lynn's life is part of Prairie City I cherish above everything else…

Alice Treat's voice was loud, penetrating. "…Prairie City will supply the new school superintendent. I understand the out-of-town candidates will not be considered this time."

It was inevitable that the subject should arise. George wished he could think of some way to kill it before it grew.

Harvey said, "They should never be, when qualified men are available here."

He rolled the slick end of his cigar between his joyous lips.

"Harvey has worked hard for the job," Alice said.

Rose could have said the same thing, George thought. But Rose was intelligent, and resourceful, and she must have sensed his secret cry, for she said to Alice, "Would you and Harvey like a game of canasta?" George knew how she hated canasta or any other pastime that had only victory for its reward.

The game was painfully slow. His usual spirit for it was dead. He had no spirit for anything but having Harvey and Alice Treat out of the house.

At nine o'clock, he was given a moderate lift when Oscar Link came in. Oscar was an editor of the Prairie City Star, and he and George had been friends for many years. George felt the impulse to remark that Oscar had saved the evening from complete ruin, and he wanted to look at Harvey as he said it.

"This isn't the sort of scene I'd expected," Oscar said after greeting everyone. "Or is my call premature?"

"You're never out of order here, Oscar," said Rose. "I was about to cook some coffee. I hope you can stay."

"I'm afraid not. I must leave as soon as I get a statement from the new superintendent of schools."

George glanced at Harvey, then at Alice and Rose. Alice started putting the cards away. Harvey was rolling a new cigar between his lips. He looked supremely pleased as he took the typewritten sheet of paper Oscar handed to him.

"Since it is official," said Oscar, "I guess I can bear the tidings."

"Would it be in bad taste to read it aloud?" said Harvey.

George felt a constriction in his throat. "By no means," he said, with altogether too much emphasis.

Harvey began with the printed title of the stationery, the date, and the salutation. George felt it was done merely to inflict pain. The voice he heard was coarse, his enunciation sloppy.

"…after long and careful consideration…"

…we have loved you with our thoughts and our hearts…

"…Mr. George Noble, principal of Clayton High School…superintendent of schools…"

At first, they were mere words to George. Then, their significance penetrated with force. He thought fleetingly of his sinfulness toward Harvey, and his mind moved swiftly toward the afternoon to recapture something he had lost in the office of Presley Edmonds.

He looked at Harvey and saw no trace of loss or disappointment on his face. These were mirrored in the eyes of Alice Treat. George sensed something akin to jubilation. He then glanced at Rose and Oscar Link, who seemed as if they had anticipated this outcome all along.

George wished strongly that Lynn could have been with him. He was confused, ashamed, yet joyous. It was not the message Harvey read. It was his attitude…He tried to remember where he had read the passage: "Mankind, while motivated by self-interest ordinarily, sometimes is capable of almost sacred generosity."

Suddenly, he felt extremely vigorous for a man of fifty.

The End

At Last Remembered

By Raymond Johnson

When she turned away from the large display window of the department store, he saw her. He stopped. He thought he had never seen a woman so lovely.

He had been walking along, dreading the thought of going back to the apartment. For the twelfth time in seventeen years, he had forgotten the anniversary present. Three days late. Five times, it was over a week, and once a full month went by. He'd go home again with a box of roses under his arm, and Louise would try to hide her disappointment. She would tell him six times how sweet the roses were, and then—

Leaving the office early, he felt drained and worn out, yearning for freedom. He longed to escape the clutter of trivial worries filling his mind. He wished he could forget the façade he and Louise were maintaining in their crowded apartment. He wanted to set aside the need to remember anniversaries, even those with Louise, if only for a while.

Then he saw this woman. It gave him a lift when she looked at him. She was beautiful. She was more than any man could expect to find standing on a street corner. Her smile was challenging. It was provocative. It belonged to the afternoon – warm, sunny, sweet with spring. It did not belong to a busy downtown street.

"A day like this shouldn't be wasted, " he said. "There's a quiet country road I know—"

The answer was in her eyes as he spoke. She made no move, but in the way she stood, the way she looked at him, there was willingness.

"My car is parked down the street," he said to her. "Shall I take a chance on your waiting – or will you come with me?"

She hooked her arm through his. He thought he felt a slight intimate squeeze.

He looked at her again. He couldn't help smiling with self-satisfaction. No one at the office would believe that he, at his age, without prearrangement, had walked into a moment so exciting with the most beautiful woman he had ever seen. He hardly believed it himself. But here he was – she beside him – and they were alive, walking, not in a dream, but down the hard concrete of Main Street.

The car was out in the country as though it had guided itself. He was hardly aware they had left the city, so fascinated was he by the childlike pleasure the woman found in the fresh new beauty of waking fields and forests.

"I have a secret place where we can have lunch," he said. "Secluded, hidden by tall sycamores—a rocky drive bordered by wild hyacinths and bluebells. Would you like that?"

She pressed herself close to him, and nodded with genuine enthusiasm.

Although his fingertips were cold, he felt warm inside, vibrant. He thought his voice trembled as he gave their order to the waiter. The woman looked about the rustic room with appreciative glances.

"This is lovely," she said softly. Her eyes lingered on his for a moment. "You're a very charming person. Meeting a man like you—that isn't what I'm really trying to say, but I don't know how to say it."

"There's something I ought to tell you," he said. "The moment I saw you, I knew this afternoon would be different. You're the most beautiful woman I've ever seen, and—Well, the trouble is I don't know how to say it either. But I'd find it very easy to make love to you."

He looked to watch her reaction, but the waiter came, and the moment was lost.

After lunch, they walked together, arm in arm, down a steep path out of the forest. They came upon a field that sloped toward a stream. She faced the wind, and breathed deeply.

"I want to run," she said, turning to him. "It's like this every time I'm in open country, where the air is light and clean."

"It used to be great fun," he laughed. "But I'm forty-two, and I'm strictly a desk man."

She took hold of his hand, and they dashed down the field together. And when they stopped near the stream, he was no worse for it than a little breathlessness. He was amazed to find he could take it. He gasped; his heart beat rapidly, but he felt young and vigorous.

They sat down on the bank at the base of a great oak, which was now beginning to leaf. Somewhere, a squirrel chattered, scolding them. The woman picked up a small stone and threw it into the brook. The sound it made was music to him. His arm stole around her, and his hand clasped hers.

She drew away a little, and he took his arm down. Perhaps he had been wrong. Perhaps this was not the afternoon that was to be unlike all the other afternoons. He had misunderstood. She had come with him only because she also had wanted to be free of something, to forget.

There was a puzzled look in her eyes when she faced him.

"I can't help it," he said. "You've done wonderful things to me this afternoon. You've taken all the stuffiness out of my forty-two years. I can't just—sit beside you when we're so close. And nothing could make me move away from you."

She didn't turn from him. She lifted her face, and the next moment, he held her firmly in his arms. He kissed her, and his kiss was not without passion.

They were secluded, concealed from the world, and even the birds had silently slipped away. The air was warm, and the earth was alive with the sweet fragrance of fresh blossoms. She rested her head in the crook of his arm, her gentle fingers tracing slowly across his face.

"I want to keep this afternoon forever," she whispered. "I'll always remember the loveliest thing you've given me since we were married."

The End

The Mother

By Raymond Johnson

Minerva Adams returned her cup to the coffee table. Her tone as she spoke was direct, without apology.

"I'm sorry I upset you. I wouldn't have said it if I weren't so upset myself. Mother's been perfectly horrid to Brian—not about him, but to him."

Edna Vincent turned from the window. She went over and sat down opposite her sister. She felt the first throb of one of her nervous headaches.

"It's almost frightening," she said. "Mother couldn't have thought such a thing about Frank. Why should she have said it—to you or to anyone?"

"Mother says a great many things that are better left unsaid. And what she thinks lives in her mind forever, even after the truth is lost in time. Her opinions of people particularly, my dear."

"She's usually right."

"Oh, so wrong, Edna," said Minerva. "Mother sits in judgment of everybody, and her judgment is based upon one point she may dislike at the moment."

Almost defiantly, Edna said, "I can't believe she said that about Frank." But even her disbelief was disturbing, for while she and her sister were alien, she had never known Minerva to be a liar.

"Forget it, darling," Minerva said. "That was fourteen years ago. With two lovely children and a comfortable home, it isn't hard to see that you and Frank have been very happy."

"That's why it frightens me. What if mother had said it to Frank? Or to me? These fourteen years may not have been, Minnie."

Her sister began putting on her gloves. "Forty and stupid. I should have kept my big mouth shut. Anyhow, you're safe from anything that can be said. Those fourteen years are under lock and key, and you stand a good chance of having three times that many more. I wish Brian and I could say that."

Edna watched the precise movements of her sister's hands as they maneuvered the tight fit of her gloves. It was strange what care she took to perform the simple act. Minnie always had been one to scoff at detail, and now she seemed amazingly attentive to trivial matters.

There were many things about her sister that Edna found strange. The two were together more frequently during the past month than at any time since she and Frank were married. Minnie had astounded everyone with the announcement that she and Brian were to be married, and she visited Edna often, as if, Edna thought, seeking moral approval of a commitment she had no right to make. Brian had been all but forgotten. No one even suspected that Minnie had revived him. Yet it seemed not something impulsive but the perfectly natural development of something long planned.

"We've been working twenty years toward a wedding," Minerva said. "It hasn't been easy. It's only because of friends like Grace Massey and my own brutal defiance that we've reached the point of hiring a church." She waved a gloved hand toward her sister.

The gesture, the intensity of her look, bore a forceful implication to Edna. She felt the involuntary stiffening of the muscle in her neck.

"I don't see how the mother can be blamed—"

"Blamed?" Minerva laughed.

Edna resented what her sister left unsaid.

"Mother and I have been very close, Minnie."

"Because you were the only one she'd allow to get that close. Even father was never quite sure where he stood. When he died, I remember – But there's no point in bringing that up. You've always been a baby to mother, Edna. You were a lovely child, and if I'd had a soft spot in me, I would have adored you."

"I used to be afraid of you, Minnie," said Edna. "You were so strong and forceful, and I used to think you considered me in your way."

"Don't get me wrong, my dear," said Minerva. "I was never jealous of you. If father had lived in place of mother, that may have been true. After he died, I thought of myself as an orphan. But I do feel now – even at my age – that it would be quite nice to have a proud parent watch me marry Brian."

"You had that once."

"Yes, how I had it. I said proud parent, darling. The first time Brian and I were married, you'd have thought we were doing something shameful in the middle of Grand Avenue. He couldn't earn a nickel to save his soul from perdition. We were willing to wait until he could, but no one else was. Well, right now, he has a good many nickels, and a hell of a lot more fortitude than he had then."

"And two other marriages behind him."

"They were part of the process, Edna. We've known it all along, and we've been patient.

"Mother never wanted to let you be hurt, Minnie."

"Hurt, indeed. If Brian had practiced twenty-four hours a day, he couldn't have been half so successful at hurting me as a mother with a single word and a vicious look. He disappointed me, but only because he threw in the sponge. He won't this time. Our marriage means a lot to me, Edna – to both of us."

Edna stood up and walked back to the window. She had never really considered marriage to be significant for a woman like Minerva Adams. To her, it always seemed that a self-sufficient woman approached marriage more as a pastime than as something essential to life. She could not grasp the significance of the marriage between Minerva and Brian. Her marriage to Frank, of course, was all-important. If it should collapse, everything… she felt the same nervous sensation of fear that had come over her earlier.

"I can't make myself believe –" she said, more to herself than to her sister, then paused.

Minerva waited, then said, "That mother spoke as she did about Frank? Well, if you insist upon nursing it – has mother ever made you aware – really feel, honestly and pleasantly – that she had accepted Frank with fondness?"

"After all, he is her son-in-law. Is she obligated to show him the affection she would a son of her own?"

"Is affection an obligation to anyone? He is entitled to something more from her than an acknowledgement of his legal right to sleep with you."

Edna faced her suddenly. "I don't like having you talk that way."

"Then I won't. I do hope you forgive me for what I've said already."

"I'm sorry I snapped at you, Minnie. I want so much to have our visits pleasant. It's been a long time since we've acted anything at all like sisters, and this month, I've grown fond of the relationship."

It was true, this fondness, but when her sister had gone, she felt, in spite of her growing headache, a great sense of relief. It was as though her nerves had been washed clean and laid in order to rest. The tension in the muscles of her side and her neck relaxed.

She cleared away the coffee cups and rearranged the cushions of the divan. From an end table, the framed picture of her husband watched her. She looked up into its gaze, and she straightened.

There was an expression on the face she had never seen before. The gaze fixed her securely. For a moment, she was troubled. Her fingers tightened in her palms…

It was ridiculous to associate any indecency with Frank, and preposterous to suspect that her mother ever had.

A sudden stab of pain tore at the left side of her head. She sank exhausted into the divan and leaned her head back. There was nothing to take anymore. This was beyond the reach of a simple sedative. It was the ten-thousandth generation of a family affliction rooted deep. All her mother's people had been plagued by incurable headaches.

The pain diminished in slow waves until it was but a vague aggravation. It filled Edna with dread of what was to come, the lassitude, the unbearable sleepiness, a series of minor pains creeping slowly across her forehead, then the heavy throbbing ache that lay like a lead band from temple to temple and increasing in intensity until the blunt stabs became blinding.

If Minnie had not come…

There was a terrible suspicion in Edna's thoughts, first of Frank, brief but wild, then of Minnie that kept struggling to free itself from her mind. Minnie certainly had a motive… There was no love between Minerva Adams and her mother, and it had not been so long as she could remember. To Minerva, mother was only an intruder. Everything the woman did in the manner of a normal mother concerned about the welfare of her children, Minerva interpreted as interference. And Minnie was jealous. She wasn't fooling anyone. Years of jealousy had built up in her, a powerful resentment toward the relationship of Edna and their mother. And it was so much stronger now, almost a passion, since Brian had been woven into the complications of her life and mother refused to accept him as she had Frank. Oh, Minnie was jealous, and she could not bear it, and the jealousy of a woman like her would not bar the most contemptible act of treachery.

Yet the suspicion remained hazy. As her headache intensified, leaving her breathless, Edna reluctantly acknowledged that Minerva, despite her harshness and occasional cruelty, had never exposed herself as an emotional fraud.

Nor had her mother, certainly. What sort of scheming trash was it that tried to make her appear as if she had? If mother had something ill to say of Frank – of anyone – she would have the courage to admit it…

Edna's headache persisted for three days. She could do nothing but lie in bed, in a darkened room, and wait for her body to wear out the pain. Then, suddenly, the pain left her. It was the morning Minerva and Grace Massey were to meet at her house to discuss the music for the wedding. She was fearfully miserable as she lay in bed contemplating the moment, and as she was about to call Minerva to have the meeting postponed, her mother called to say she was coming over. Less than an hour later, she felt the swift recession of pain, and the relief, like cool water to a parched throat, was sweet and invigorating.

Grace Massey, a dark woman of forty-five, dressed with the crisp, harsh perfection of a meticulous businesswoman, was having coffee with Edna when Mrs. Chalmers Adams arrived.

She made a striking appearance; Edna noted this proudly as she hugged her. She did not look as if she had been engaged in a serious argument. She was calm, composed, and not without dignity. At sixty-five she had the carriage of a woman thirty years younger and, except for an unbecoming looseness of flesh beneath her chin, no less beauty.

Mrs. Chalmers Adams was cool to the introduction of Grace Massey. "Yes, Minerva has spoken of you – a great deal." Only once Minerva had spoken of her, but Mrs. Chalmers Adams found it easier to imply with her speech that Minnie had complained about her as a condition. She put down her packages and took off her coat.

"I have some things for the children." She said as she unwrapped her gifts.

"No, mother, you shouldn't have!" Edna exclaimed. "It isn't good for them to have such expensive things." But as she turned to Grace, her delight was easy to see. "Mother is determined to do to the girls what she thought wrong for me and Minnie."

When Mrs. Chalmers Adams spoke, it was as if Edna were the only other person present. "Now that every hour is precious to me, my dear, I'm indulging to the limit." With effective emphasis, she added, "I know how hard it is for Frank to make ends meet in these days of high taxes and ridiculous prices."

Edna's glance toward Grace Massey was too quick to conceal her embarrassment.

As if attempting to put her at ease, Grace Massey said, "The trouble for a man with a family isn't so much in making ends meet as it is in achieving a heartening overlap."

Mrs. Chalmers Adams did not acknowledge the remark. She grasped her daughter by the arms.

"Child, look at me. You've been dragging through another of your miserable headaches. Why didn't you let me know?"

"I didn't want to upset you, mother. And I feel wonderful today."

"Frank should make you see a doctor," said her mother as she gathered together the package wrappings. "He shouldn't let you suffer year after year as you do."

"Oh, Frank doesn't make me suffer. I'm perfectly free to see a doctor any time I choose."

"Why don't you then? You need someone to help you through. Is Frank afraid of the bill, Edna?"

"Mother, I've been to doctors. It's always the same simple remedy – relax and quit fretting. How does a woman with two children and a husband relax, and when can she quit fretting?"

"If you only had someone to help you with the house."

"That would be someone else to fret about," said Edna. "Now forget me and have a cup of fresh coffee. Or would you rather wait for Minnie?"

Her mother faced her. "I don't think Minerva is coming," she said.

Edna glanced toward Grace Massey.

"Yes," her mother said, "she told me she was to meet Miss Massey. But before I left her she became involved in one of those bristling business affairs of hers. You know Minerva, Miss Massey – the supreme executive at all times, even in the face of her own wedding."

Edna Vincent then observed in her mother what she had not seen at first, and when Grace Massey had gone, she said, "It's not like Minnie to do that to Grace, mother."

"Minerva knew I was coming here," her mother answered.

"She should have called."

Mrs. Chalmers Adams sipped at her coffee. Minerva was too angry to care about formality." She watched her daughter over the rim of her cup. "As usual, she was angry with me."

"I've been wishing so much lately that you and Minerva could make peace."

"Make peace, indeed," her mother said in exasperation. "My dear, I've tried. I admit I made a mistake this afternoon. I criticized her for wearing that awful perfume of hers."

"But, mother, if she likes it –"

"Oh. She can't possibly like it. Twenty years ago, perhaps, but Minerva knows by now that she isn't a coquette."

"She has certain points that need accenting," said Edna.

"And a great many more that gay perfume won't subdue." She put down her cup. "I didn't mean to start an argument that covered everything from her perfume to Brian's new house. But that's what happened. You simply can't talk to Minerva with honesty."

"Since her wedding is so near, I'd hoped that all these trivial things between you could be forgotten. Not that I think you're wrong, mother –"

"No," her mother said, and she looked at her sternly. "No, not that, Edna. I am wrong about so many things. I have been wrong before, but I do try – very hard, dear – to correct myself." Her features softened as she said, "Trivial things. There is no such thing as triviality in Minerva's life. Whatever concerns her is of utmost importance."

"Yes, I know, mother. And I think her wedding is important, much more than we realize." She went over to her mother and put her arms about her neck. "Why does it seem so awful to you?"

Her mother's hand clasped hers gently. "My dear, the idea isn't ugly. I'm sorry I've given you that impression. I must remind you, it hasn't been long since you thought it rather silly."

Edna rose and walked to the window. "Not silly, but odd – for Minnie. Now, it seems rather nice."

"Nice, Edna? Have you considered how she's going about it? It's being vulgarly overdone. Church – flowers—music – gowns – bridesmaids – over two hundred guests. It isn't as if romance were the prime factor. It has the appearance of immoral mockery. If she must marry Brian, why can't she do it quietly and simply in a parsonage? Why must she implicate me in this grandstand performance that lacks very little to make it resemble a grotesque political rally."

Edna was silent for a few seconds, then she said abruptly, "You let me have the experience Minnie has always wanted to have. Didn't you, mother?"

"Your wedding was in good taste, Edna."

Edna turned and walked slowly to stand before her mother.

"You trusted Frank to preserve the happiness I knew at that moment, didn't you, mother?"

Mrs. Chalmers Adams picked up her cup again. "Between Minerva and Brian, happiness can be of no consideration." It has been the only consideration between Frank and me," Edna replied, her voice tinged with a rising sense of desperation, as if she were grasping for something just out of reach. She sat down again, facing her mother, and as she clasped her hands, she noticed her knuckles turning white from the pressure of her twisting fingers.

Brian has a reputation that stalks him everywhere he goes," her mother said. "Minerva will be no more than a social shield for him because his profession demands a background of domestic stability." She sipped the last of her coffee. "How it survived in its past environment is a mystery to me."

Edna looked down at her hands. "Frank had no need for such a shield. There can be no doubt that he wanted only the simple wholesomeness of a home and family."

"The picture of Brian being devoted to either home or family escapes me completely."

Edna felt her face grow hot as the familiarity of the words struck her.

"I never thought him unkind or unpleasant," she said stiffly, raising her head.

"A man's stature is more than demeanor, Edna. Brians' is not. He can have no moral regard for Minerva, none whatever. Frankly, Edna, Brian's a fiend."

"Oh, mother—" Edna said weakly.

She felt it again, the nervous tenseness which had followed Minerva's visit, the tightening of tissue and muscle, the knotting and twisting, and the confined spastic trembling in scattered areas of her body.

"Can it be? Is it true?" And she was not sure if her questions were put to her mother about Brian or to herself about her mother.

"Of course, it's true," her mother replied emphatically. "And he will not sacrifice one moment of his pleasures for Minerva. You may depend upon that, Edna."

"It's so ugly, mother," said Edna.

Mrs. Chalmers Adams put her empty cup on the table and watched her daughter's face.

"I almost wish this wedding could not take place," said Edna.

She felt the first faint throb of pain in her left temple.

"Mother, you're always so right about people. Frank and I—we were well suited, weren't we?

Her mother said nothing.

Edna faced her suddenly. "Have you ever feared that Frank would be unfaithful to me?"

Mrs. Chalmers Adams sat forward stiffly and looked at her severely. "Why, child, whatever are you trying to tell me?"

Edna's hands relaxed and lay limp in her lap. "Nothing, mother."

"You've something on your mind, Edna."

"No, mother. I Only wanted to be sure of your trust."

"Whatever made you suspect it? How could anyone doubt Franks's fidelity?"

Edna leaned her head back, and while the next throb of pain was more intense, there was also some pleasure in it.

"I only wanted to know, mother. That's all." And as she gave herself up to the new agony that was taking possession of her, she was comforted by the knowledge that Minerva was a liar.

Although she spent two days in bed, her new headache was less severe. Frank had urged her to rest so there would not be another relapse. Frank was a dear, she reflected frequently, and she was extremely fortunate to have a husband so true. There was no doubt in her mind that he was exceptionally devoted to her, and her security was fortified by her mother's expressed conviction of it. "How could anyone doubt Frank's fidelity?" She had said it so directly and honestly that she was completely vindicated of Minerva's foolish charge. Poor Minnie. It was easy to see now that there was desperation in everything she did.

It was pathetic, this desperation. Mother had made it so clear. Minnie always had repulsed the tenderest advances of life, and now she reached for them with cruel disregard for anyone she believed was opposed to her. Mother was not opposed to her, but to the circus performance she was making of her wedding. Mother detested bad manners…

She said this to Frank one evening several days later. She did not know it would be a prelude to the severest headache she had ever suffered.

"Your mother detests bad manners in other people," Frank had said calmly.

She meant to say no more, but the weight of his unjust implication was tremendous. She became angry, but Frank remained unimpassioned as he talked to her.

"Why should it be so disgusting for two people to get married?" he asked. "Edna, it's more than that. You were pleased by the idea when Minnie first told you. Then, something happened to make it seem repulsive. You've suffered one miserable headache after another. It's not the wedding –"

"NO, not the wedding," she said heatedly. "You think Mother's been a meddling, interfering fool."

He had tried to remain silent after that, but she was relentless, pushing him until he was compelled to respond. He seized her wrists, holding them firmly.

"You'd make your mother happy if she could see how miserable you are at this moment, Edna. She's tried to make Minnie unhappy and can't bear it because she's failed. Don't give her victory, Edna."

"You and Minnie!" she cried. "You're trying to make a mother out of a fraud and a cheat."

She twisted her wrists free and stepped away from him. "You would believe Minnie before mother. You would believe Minnie before Mother. You would believe the lies she claimed mother said about you."

Frank had pleaded with her to compose herself, but only the shock of his losing patience with her was stabilizing.

"You spoke of manners," he said sharply. "What about your mother's? Has she always considered me when she's done things she thought nice for us? I am your husband. Your welfare is my responsibility. Yet in every situation where I should assume it, your mother insists that I have made no effort to find out what causes your headaches. I have done what I can. She wouldn't believe me if I told her you refused to see a good doctor because you abhorred the thought of having your bowels explored."

"Oh, Frank, stop it."

"I don't think I should, Edna. Your mother is determined to be the focal point of all activity within her sphere. She showers gifts upon the children—expensive ones. What ten-year-old girl has any business with a sterling silver dresser set? A cheap doll will buy more affection than that."

He relented when she became pale and trembling from nervous exhaustion, and though he was commiserative, her furious resentment kept mounting as her pain grew in intensity. He helped her to bed, and she had remained there until the day before Minnie's wedding, agonized by the thoughts which made violent thrusts of doubt and confusion into her mind.

Perhaps Minnie had not lied, after all. Perhaps Mother had said those things about Frank, and perhaps they were true, and Mother denied saying them only to save her anguish and humiliation. There was no way of knowing the truth....

She must believe Frank, or her entire world would shatter. But how? He had admitted nothing, denied nothing. He had said only, "It's unimportant what your mother may have said about me, Edna. My concern is for you, your health—your happiness—"

Her mother came the afternoon before the wedding. Edna was sitting in the living-room, wrapped in her robe. Frank was home, and he had just brought in a tray of toast and tea when the mother arrived.

The woman was harried and nervous, and her concern for her daughter seemed exaggerated.

"You poor, dear child. How you have suffered. Let me put these pillows behind you and make you more comfortable."

Edna protested, but her mother took her way. She turned to Frank, who stood by the fireplace.

"Frank, you must do something for this child. I can't bear the thought of her suffering any longer."

"I wouldn't worry about her if I were you," he said.

She fixed a firm gaze upon him. "No," she said, "you wouldn't. But I do."

"There's nothing to be alarmed about, Mother," said Edna. "I've made an appointment with a good doctor. Now have a cup of tea with me and relax."

"I haven't time for that, my dear," her mother said, turning to her. "I must go as soon as I've caught my breath. Minerva has just about set me wild."

Frank walked to the center of the room and faced Mrs. Chalmers Adams.

"Edna is getting over a severe attack," he said. "Lately, the mere mention of Minerva has upset her. Unless it's necessary, let's not talk about Minerva this afternoon."

Mrs. Chalmers Adams drew herself erect, clasping her fingers in front of her.

"Well, I should say you've become suddenly very considerate. It certainly is necessary after what I've been through. For the past two days, I've done nothing but call wedding guests on the telephone."

"What on earth for?" Edna cried. "What has happened?"

Mrs. Chalmers Adams flung her hands out to her sides in a gesture of desperation. "Minerva probably thinks it's nothing. To her, it would seem just good business to decide suddenly to change the wedding from the church to Brian's house."

Frank shrugged, and turned back to the fireplace. "Well, I guess that would lower the boom."

"Why, Mother, it's absurd," Edna exclaimed. "Two hundred guests—Why, the house won't hold half of them."

Her mother strode over to her. "I don't care. I don't care one bit, Edna. That's her problem. I'm through with the whole thing. This time tomorrow, I'll be on my way to Florida, and I'll be pleased— very pleased – if I never set eyes on Minerva again."

Edna slumped back into her chair, closing her eyes as if in silent resignation to the coming day. She struggled to keep her body still, determined not to let any unsettling thoughts take hold. But what Minerva had done seemed utterly insane!

When her mother had gone Frank moved into the bedroom. Edna followed him. She felt weak and empty, needing him for strength, to free her of the sordidness that had enveloped her.

"Frank – Frank, I can't go to the wedding. I couldn't bear it."

He took her in his arms. "I know, darling. I don't blame you. There's only one more day – then you can forget."

The telephone in the hall rang, and she went to answer it. She came back pale; her lips ash color.

"Grace Massey," she said feebly.

She could scarcely make her feet carry her to the bed. Frank took her by the arm and supported her.

"Mother has the list of guests," she said. "Grace wants me to try to get it."

She sat down on the bed, Frank beside her.

"Frank – Minnie – Frank, there was never any change—in the wedding plans—"

The End

Hollow Time

By Raymond Johnson

When Sam Wood entered the living room of his house its stillness was like a web he had walked through unsuspecting. It was temporary, and he knew it would be brief, but it was disagreeable while it lasted. So many moments have been like this lately.

He tossed his hat onto the coffee table and reluctantly lit a cigarette. The moment was long, and the smoke from his cigarette was harsh.

His wife came in from the patio at the rear of the house. She greeted him cheerfully, and kissed him dutifully.

"You're a few minutes early this evening, and you look tired. Anything wrong?"

He shook his head. "The usual planless, voiceless drudgery. Where are the children?"

"At Romney's. Edna's mother gave her a birthday party after school. I don't like their having refreshments so near dinner time, but I guess there's nothing I can do about it."

This was the attitude she was taking so often lately about matters concerning the children.

"Alice –" he said, then he thought better of it. He had told her how he felt, many times. It was becoming too easy for her to give in to them.

"Yes, darling?" she said.

"Oh – never mind." He turned toward the divan, sat down, and leaned his head back. "Don't hurry dinner on my account. I'm not hungry."

"But I'd planned an early one," she said. "Charles and Ellen are coming afterward for canasta."

"Funny, Charles didn't mention it at the office."

"I doubt if he knew," his wife said as she started toward the kitchen. At the doorway, she paused and faced him. "Ellen called this afternoon to tell me about her new coat. I think she cooked up the evening to show it off."

When she had gone, Sam shifted his body in search of a more comfortable position. A hard object prodded him. He reached under his leg and removed Tom's water pistol, a remnant of Alice's last of a thousand circuits of the house to recover a boy's neglected possessions. He settled back again and closed his eyes.

Alone in the room again, he felt the remaining part of the web.

It was the absence of the children. He liked having them home when he arrived. They gave him something fresh and clean and honest to look upon at the end of a savage day. Even on those cataclysmic days when they aggravated him and Alice to the point of hysteria, it was easy for him to soften with tolerance. They would remain, always and forever, no matter what else he lost. His redeeming asset.

A man's children are an expression of his ego; they mirror his vanity.

As the thought skipped through his mind, he wondered whom his subconscious was quoting.

He secretly, silently, boasted to himself, now as in many daydreams at his desk, of possessing them. They were of his body, of his mind, and their creation was a noble achievement. This was solace for mediocrity.

Andover's, Incorporated, was barren. It was rich and old and withered. It was a dirty brick shell containing foundry dirt, machinery, green packing lumber, old men, and fruitless women. And his desk. His desk, his hopes, his dreams, his fears.

It was very satisfying to know that he alone among the exempt salaried men, those cryptoclastic creatures of industry, had two children still to bloom and cherish. Old Man Andover, of course, had three sons, but they were all vice presidents stained by middle-age and enslaved by cardiographs. But Sam never had fondled the hope of emulating the Old Man. Disregarding progeny, there always would be a difference of three million dollars.

Charles Forsythe had no children. He and Ellen lived strictly for themselves, loving children dearly but bearing none, preferring to have their habits and customs uncluttered by this interfering love. Gil Sampler, for thirty years Andover's production manager, had five, but all five had added time with Gil, though not his wisdom, had left him to become famous and vanished among the nation's averages.

Sam Wood observed his children with a timeless regard. They would grow older, but never become old, never dissolve in the statistical mixture which produced the hollowness of the Sam Woods in offices like Andover's…

He was starting to drift off, lulled by the distant sound of children's laughter—though they weren't his, and a Romney cake sat nearby. In the kitchen, Alice moved about, the clatter and hum of her work clear and sharp, but he was only vaguely aware that it was her or that the noises he heard belonged to her. There was a brightness to semi-sleep, a grey brightness like a dense cloud catching the rays of evening sun on its belly. There was a passage in his mind an oblong of this grey brightness through which a great draft of air unheard or unfelt pushed its way and filled with a peculiar arrangement of the faces of Gil Sampler, Charles Forsythe, Old Man Andover, and his own children. He was in their midst, aloof, speaking toward the end of the passage. "Other men at Andover's calculate their wealth; Sam Wood evaluates his." His voice was loud, as if shouted into a sound box, but the words had a stirring clarity, and he was about to repeat them when Alice came into the room and lifted him out of the dip.

"You'd better get cleaned up," she said. "There won't be time after dinner."

He sat forward and rubbed his face with his hands.

"Did you hear what I said?"

She shook her head.

"I thought I was talking when you woke me."

"You must have been dreaming," she said and turned to go back to the kitchen.

She said more in her flight, but its coherence was lost somewhere in the distance between him and the sink. It was something about Ellen's penchant for bragging without uttering a word. Ellen was bad that way, Sam reflected. By her manners alone, she impressed everyone with her conviction that Charles was the rising star at the plant. She was, from head to toe, a walking symbol of Charlie's success.

Sam thought such conduct would be embarrassing, but Charlie seemed to bask in his wife's vanity. It had its effect on the women in their circle, however. They were beginning to show resentment. Not to Ellen, of course, because they were still uncertain whether she cared.

Stirring himself from the nest his relaxing body had made in the divan, Sam wondered if there were enough cold beer for the evening. Perhaps cocktails would be more appropriate for the Forsythe's now, but at his house, they would have to be satisfied with beer. He thought about checking the refrigerator's inventory but discarded the idea.

"They can afford to buy their own if there's not enough," he said to himself.

The process of grinding off the day's dirt and whiskers would be a chore this evening, for he wanted no company other than that of his own family. He had come home unexplainably tired in body, hoping to spend a few minutes with the children, have dinner, read the paper, watch the telecast of the fights, and go to bed. Instead, he had entered the silent house, a chasm of exclusion, and let himself slide easily into a depression.

Six o'clock melancholy, he called it, a state of mind that followed him home from the office periodically. It would trail him without his suspecting it; then, as he reached the living room of his house, it would catch up with him, gnaw its way into a low area, and lay its eggs of distress. There was nothing mysterious about it. He knew its identity. It was, of course, basically a combination of fragments from each of his forty-two years. But its main body was composed of the last five years at Andover's, its nucleus forming the day he entered the competition for the big jobs.

He had spent ten years at rather nameless jobs, willingly because he anticipated the reward of hope. Then, his restlessness overwhelmed him with an almost violent urge to make his name of significance to Andover's Incorporated. He made progress, but it was not rapid, and it was not easy. Gil Planter had pulled for him, but even with Gil's help, he was always going uphill, a runner without shoes.

Sam was never sure where he stood. For twenty-five years of his life, he had applied the principles he had learned were essential to success, but at forty-two, he had no greater feeling of achievement than the new mail clerk. Less. He possessed the knowledge, the ability, the energy, and his philosophy always had included loyalty, uprightness, and punctuality, but there was a lack he could not supply. He was by no means a personality boy with the knack of selling sawdust stuffing as gold dust.

The melancholy had come over him more frequently during the past three months. When he found out Gil Sampler was retiring, he made a bid for the job. He was next in line for it. Gil wanted him to have it. He spoke to Old Man Andover, and the old man listened to him quite respectfully, and when he finished talking, Andover said only "There's plenty of time to think about it."

If any thinking was done Sam never knew. The usual rule that office rumor is the smell of the fire did not apply. If Andover's officers had made any decision about Gil Sampler's job, it was a closely guarded secret.

"It will have to come out soon," Sam said to his mirrored reflection as he brushed lather on his face. "Only ten more days for Gil."

He thought about talking to Andover in the morning and having the matter settled. His doubt and fear and the suspense had rotted his office time, and it had begun rotting his leisure, and he was not the man he had envisioned at seventeen or at twenty-seven when he boasted to Alice about his future. Establishing a certainty one way or the other would be better.

But he knew he was afraid to establish that certainty.

He swished his razor through the bowl of hot water, and he wondered why he had been doing so much primping lately for

Charlie Forsythe. He and Charlie had been friends for many years and neither had demanded a meticulous appearance of the other on informal occasions.

"Charlie's changed," he said as he made a small o with his mouth and shaved around the edges. Charlie was a climber now. Ellen's influence. They were growing farther apart. Soon, Ellen would have Charlie weaned away from him entirely. The Sam Woods had nothing to offer Ellen Forsythe.

Charlie wanted Gil's job and made no secret about it. His intense desire glowed like a phosphorescent coating. He even confessed to Sam that, while he might not know what to do with the role if he got it, the desire was too strong to ignore. Charlie needed the job for a reason different from Sam's. It was a matter of prestige to him, not a principle of meeting a challenge to test the strength and endurance of his character. To Charlie, promotions were like a varnish to the grain of wood; they simply prepared him for the environment he preferred.

As he cleaned the excess lather from his face, Sam looked grimly at himself in the mirror.

"You're jealous. And for three months, you've had half a conviction Charlie'd get the job you want."

Alice was tapping on the bathroom door. "Dinner in about ten minutes. The children won't be home. Mrs. Romney called and asked if they could have dinner with Edna."

Sam opened the door, drying his face.

"Ready except for my shirt," he said and went into the bedroom.

Children at Romney's. It seemed to him suddenly that they were always somewhere. Only fourteen and ten, and already their time was being consumed by obligations. He disliked, more intensely at this moment than any other, the feeling of subordination to his household. He was becoming, all at once, a smaller part of his children's life. Not that he would have objected to their staying at Romney's, but he would have liked the opportunity to agree, to be a part of their plans, their fun as well as their discipline. He always looked forward to the dinner table with the children present, even though, too often, the only influence he could exercise at dinner time was corrective. Alice, naturally, had to make most of the decisions, but…

"Sam," she said at the door.

He turned. "Oh, I thought you had gone."

"Did you hear what I said?"

"No, I must have been wool-gathering."

"The cashier at Levinson's Department Store –"there was a frown in her hesitation. "He called this morning. Your check was returned."

"Returned? Why—" Then he remembered.

"I told him there must have been a mix-up at the bank," she said, "and to re-deposit the check. Was that the thing to do?"

"Yes – yes, that was the thing to do."

The frown vanished. "Banks seldom make a mistake, but it's awfully embarrassing when they do," Alice said.

She left to return to the kitchen.

He buttoned his shirt, watching the precise mechanical movement of the man in the mirror as his necktie slid smoothly under the starched collar, rolled into silken adornment, and slipped snugly into place to conceal the flesh sag of the throat.

The bank had not made a mistake. It had been a small gamble of his with time…

He followed Alice to the kitchen.

"The money was not in the bank, Alice," he said. There was a brief flight of alarm in her eyes. "It's all right now. My deposit was only a day late—"

"And they couldn't have held your check one day?" She passed him and placed the butter on the table. "You've been a customer for thirteen years, and they know your deposits are regular."

"The money wasn't there," he repeated.

She stopped and looked at him with a trace of resentment.

"Are banks above little favors for their regular customers?"

"Their regular little customers," he said. He carried the bread plate to the table. "Maybe it's a question of economics—and a little sociology. Favoring large accounts is good business. But I'm only Sam Wood, forty-two, one of the millions of white-collar men with a home, a family–waning hope and limited potential. Why should a bank favor me?"

He briefly saw the woman, his wife.

"I'm sorry, darling," he said. "I was quoting statistical records. They're tragic only when given specific application."

She stepped closer to him and placed her hands upon his arms.

"Sam—did you know the check would bounce?"

"I closed my eyes and hoped it wouldn't beat my deposit."

"Is there something wrong, Sam?"

"No – nothing unusual." He helped her finish setting the table. "It's just that the pace of living—prices, taxes, ambition—is much swifter than Sam Wood."

"We're not extravagant, Sam."

He shook his head but said nothing. There were extravagances, little, incalculable ones which by themselves were insignificant but which, added together, became painful in their collective uselessness. There were knick-knacks for the house, never seen, never admired, without meaning; household articles which came by way of slick advertising and never seemed to merit the standard of performance boasted; things for the children stuffed in a drawer, lost in a forgotten corner of a closet; his own golf clubs, used four times last year and then only half-heartedly; the sewing machine Alice bought so she could economize on the children's clothing--idle.

And there were those dinners he bought for Andover, his three sons, and Gil Sampler – sheer waste. He had wasted money on high priced steaks because he thought it was the thing to do. He was trying to sell himself to Gil's job. He was being sociable with an ulterior motive. Charlie Forsythe had told him once that he was too much of a recluse and needed to socialize more with the influential crowd. However, when he tried to engage with people like Andover—the ones who mattered—he found his efforts awkward and underwhelming.

Long after Alice was seated, he reiterated what she had said. "But," he added, "it's possible we're not extravagant enough."

She looked up at him, but he avoided her eyes.

"Behavior, Alice," he said. "Some of us are very stingy with what we have under our capable, efficient surface. It's what makes the difference between charm and dullness. The office man without charm these days is like a woman wrestler in a beauty parade."

Alice treated his remarks lightly. "With men, at least, hips and legs don't have to be a consideration."

Both then were silent. Presently, Alice said, "Have you heard anything from Mr. Andover?"

"No."

"It's been bothering you a great deal lately. Having important questions left unanswered for so long makes one wish they'd never been asked."

Yes, it had bothered him, and he knew she had felt the anguish of waiting. He wondered if Old Man Andover knew the torture his silence held. It would have been better, for Alice as well as for him, if Andover had said at once, or perhaps no more than a month later, that other arrangements had been made. The element of cruelty would have been removed. Man, of course, finds pleasure in some form of cruelty, and the polite cruelty of the executive may have been gratifying to Andover.

It would be more bitter if he should learn that Charlie Forsythe had known the answer before this. Charlie was with Andover a great deal socially, and it was not unreasonable to think that Andover, during a moment of tactlessness, may have confided in him.

Sam bore no resentment against Charlie. The man wanted old Sampler's job and had every right to try for it. He was green. He had moved around Andover's plant too rapidly to absorb any part of it. This was not Charlie's fault. He was scarcely dirty from his first job, checking and counting molds in the foundry ten years ago, when he was moved to a desk in the shop timekeeper's office. His good looks, his naivete, his glib tongue, and his smooth manner attracted attention. Sam became aware of him when he was moved into the front office. He liked him. It was not possible to dislike Charlie. Sam helped him when an assignment proved to be a little too much for him, and Charlie's dependence on him became the basis for their friendship.

Charlie was a hard worker, but so much of his effort was dissipated in meaningless directions. He was a great one for systems. He was forever dreaming up a new one. His ideas for them made good conversation and stood up well on paper, but by the time details were worked out his plans of procedure were so bulky they collapsed of their own weight.

Sam got the impression that Charlie's energy did not spring from a deep well, that it had to be forced up and projected. It seemed, not only to Sam but to other men in the office, that Charlie's primary concern was not with what he was doing but whom he was doing it for. Once promoted to the front office, he kept looking for the right guy, and it was not long before Old Man Andover, and Andover alone, bore the tag.

No one at Andover's, Sam though, could say honestly that Charlie looked like the man for Gil's job. Gil was an artist in organization and production, and he looked the part. Sometimes, it's easy to spot a bond salesman by his looks, or a bank clerk, a salesman of insurance, or a bus driver, but looking at Charlie, one received only a good impression. He could be identified with nothing closer to a profession or skill than a Phi Beta Kappa who had left his car keys at home and needed a free ride.

Sam was not happy with his thinking at the moment, and suddenly, it occurred to him that he was not eating. He looked at Alice. She was smiling.

"I'm sorry, dear," he said. "It isn't the food. I'm simply not hungry."

"And not listening," she said. "You didn't hear a word I said. I asked if it was terribly important what sort of decision Mr. Andover makes."

He thought a moment. "Yes. To a man, Alice, it is very important to know whether he's a success."

"But if Mr. Andover doesn't give you Gil's job, does it mean you've failed at the one you have?"

He figured she had come to terms with the inevitable and was now trying to ease the burden on him. It was her nature—the wife, the mother—shielding him from the harsh reality. She had wanted Gil's job for him as much as he had. The additional money would have meant a great deal more to her than to him. She must have schemed a thousand times during the past three months how it was to be allocated – the children, the house, her own wardrobe, all must have been treated generously in her anticipation. But more than the money was involved. The real thing was what he saw in her eyes, pride and admiration. They were genuine and tender, and his failure would hurt. It would be a deep hurt. He could see how deep as he looked at her smile, as he reflected how patient she had been, never once pushing him with persuasion to back Andover into a corner for a showdown.

"Alice," he said, falteringly because time had fled swiftly since the last time he said the word. "Alice—you're lovely."

She gave him a look of real pleasure.

"Because you're not hungry?"

"No." he reached over and put his hand on hers, and for the first time since he reached home, he found it easy to be pleasant. "No, I suddenly felt it – so I said it."

"It's very nice, Sam."

The End

www.ingramcontent.com/pod-product-compliance
Lightning Source LLC
Chambersburg PA
CBHW051557030726

47592CB00001B/328